Advance Praise
The Value-Driven Business Analyst

Business analysis is a critical skill for all software professionals, and it's one of the few that will survive the changes being wrought by AI. This book provides the skills and knowledge that you need to remain competitive in your career.

—Scott Ambler,
Author, *Agile Modeling and The Objective Primer,* 3rd Edition

When I began my journey to become a Salesforce Business Analyst over 15 years ago, Laura Brandenburg's work was my guidepost. At a time when few resources existed that spoke to the day-to-day realities of the role, Laura's blog and first book, *How to Start a Business Analyst Career,* gave me the practical insights and templates I needed to visualize the career I wanted—and ultimately built.

Today, as the founder of *Systems To Success,* I teach that there are no secrets to success—but there *are* systems. Laura's 8-Step Business Process is that system. It gives business analysts a clear, sequential roadmap they can apply to any project, in any environment, to consistently deliver value and drive alignment.

In *The Value-Driven Business Analyst,* Laura has once again created a resource that not only equips BAs with proven techniques, but also builds their confidence as leaders and change agents. Her ability to simplify complex processes into actionable steps is unparalleled.

If you've ever doubted your skills, struggled with imposter syndrome, or lacked confidence in your approach—this book is your blueprint to becoming the impactful, value-driven BA you were meant to be.

—Toni V. Martin, ACBA,
Founder, Systems To Success

The Value-Driven Business Analyst turns business analysis into something practical, clear, and truly actionable—**Laura Brandenburg's experience shines through,** making it an invaluable guide for anyone looking to create real impact through BA work.

—Fabricio Laguna,
The Brazilian BA

Laura has created an excellent "how to" guide for business analysis professionals, whether new to the role or well established, looking to refine their skills.

One of the most challenging aspects of business analysis is getting started on new assignments, scoping, identifying and analyzing stakeholders, and planning the business analysis work needed. Laura addresses this with **practical advice, providing specific examples of starting questions and actions—even for situations where the analyst is brought onto the team late in the process**—which can be used to dive into the work. She correctly stresses the importance of clear communications and expectation setting.

Her willingness to admit vulnerabilities will build the confidence of business analysis professionals who occasionally feel vulnerable when starting work on an unfamiliar business area or solution.

Many important business analysis techniques are covered along with advantages and disadvantages of each and suggestions of when they might be useful. I highly recommend this book to readers of all levels wanting to increase their confidence and skill set in this important profession.

—Barbara Carkenord, CBAP, PMP, IIBA-AAC, PMI-PBA, PMI-ACP
Senior Consultant

Laura Brandenburg's new book is an essential and practical guide for business analysts eager to elevate their impact and career trajectory. Drawing on her rich personal experience, Laura offers a clear, linear roadmap filled with **actionable techniques that empower analysts to become more strategic, proactive, and confident contributors within their organizations.** It encourages business analysts to become key drivers of strategic alignment and business value, and to embrace leadership and influence at every stage of their professional journey.

This book is a must-read for anyone committed to the craft of business analysis to drive meaningful change and career advancement.

—Dr. Tracie Edwards,
Founder of Traceability Coaching,
and host of the Traceability podcast

Simply stated, **this book is comprehensively packed with Business Analysis techniques that really work.**

I know that's true because I've used many of those techniques myself during my 30 years as a business analyst. They range from the technical (such as how to rigorously capture a business's most important concepts) all the way to the sociological (such as how to handle a set of disparate stakeholders with conflicting needs).

Laura's actually done the stuff that she writes about in this book. Her authenticity leaps from the page, because only people who have wrestled with real projects would know the insider tips that Laura gives you in this book.

If you're starting out as a business analyst, you'll find this book valuable to ease yourself into what initially looks to be a difficult and daunting career. **It will reassure you that what you're doing is right, even when you sometimes doubt yourself.**

Laura's book is also a great reference for experienced analysts. I enjoyed seeing the jumble of facts, skills and techniques that I've haphazardly acquired over the years laid out in an orderly way. Beyond that, I learned several new approaches that I'm eager to apply.

—Meilir Page-Jones,
Author, *The Practical Guide to Structured Systems Design*

Well-structured and easy to navigate. Throughout the book Laura's passion for business analysis shines through. She has provided a practical guide for business analysts, whether they are experienced or new to the role. This is a brilliant new resource for the BA community.

—Christina Lovelock,
Business Analysis Leader, Coach and Author

If you add one new book to your collection this year, make sure it's *The Value-Driven Business Analyst*. **This is a practical guide that is the very definition of what makes a BA great.** From the very start, encouraging us to slow down to speed up and being unapologetic about taking the time to get oriented and discover the primary business goals before rushing into requirements gathering. This is just the beginning of a brilliantly crafted guide; it goes on to clearly explain numerous great paths through the wonderful world of business analysis.

Particularly impressive is the book's contemporary relevance, with each section offering practical suggestions for integrating AI into Business Analysis workflows to enhance efficiency and value creation. This forward-thinking approach ensures the text won't quickly become outdated in our rapidly evolving technological environment. The additional downloadable templates and supplementary materials extend the book's usability beyond its pages, providing readers with immediate tools to implement its principles.

—Linda Parker,
Senior Business Analyst, CEO of BA Life

This actionable, practical book is full of techniques and success strategies for becoming the kind of business analyst that makes a strategic difference (and earns a salary to match). Laura Brandenburg's advice is a goldmine for anyone who wants to become a high performing business analyst—**the chapter on the BA plan alone will make a**

difference to how you are perceived at work. The tried-and-tested blueprint is an easy-to-follow route to contributing effectively, making a real difference on projects and enjoying your job.

—Elizabeth Harrin,
Author, *Managing Multiple Projects*

If your success depends on understanding what stakeholders need (not just what they ask for), this is essential reading. With ready-to-use talk tracks, templates, and a proven process, Laura Brandenburg guides you through uncovering actual business needs, aligning diverse perspectives, and delivering meaningful solutions. Whether working in agile teams, developing custom solutions, or implementing SaaS, this book provides adaptable frameworks to help you excel in your role.

—Jodi Hrbek
Author, *Rock Your Role as a Salesforce Admin*

This book is a highly practical and pragmatic resource that I would recommend without hesitation to any business analyst, regardless of experience level. It offers a flexible, repeatable framework that can be adapted depending on the delivery life cycle or organizational context.

One thing I particularly liked is its clear recognition of the variety in BA roles and environments, steering away from a prescriptive approach in favor of guidance that readers can tailor to their own situations.

Each chapter concludes with actionable 'next steps,' making it easy for readers to apply what they've learned. The integration of AI into business analysis is addressed in a grounded, thoughtful way, with tips embedded throughout the book rather than treated as a standalone topic.

The inclusion of mini case studies and the author's own experiences (both successes and challenges) adds valuable context. There's also a strong focus on appreciating the breadth of the BA role (from defining outcomes to determining whether those outcomes were met), as well as ensuring the BA role is visible and appreciated.

It's clear that this book was written by someone with deep, hands-on experience and a true understanding of the BA mindset. It is a highly useful, relevant, and adaptive guide.

—Adrian Reed,
Principal Consultant at Blackmetric, Editor-in-Chief at BA Digest

This newest book by Laura Brandenburg is THE BASIS for understanding the actions and goals of being a Business Analyst. Not only does she give you the concepts, but also stories and explanations you can take each into your own workplace immediately. This is a MUST READ for those interested in being better BAs!

—Thea Soehren, CBAP,
President, Tampa Bay, Florida IIBA Chapter
and Founder, BA Force Multiplier

Laura does a fantastic job of guiding, coaching, and supporting Business Analysts at all stages of their journey, and this book brings all of that together. It's a must-read for Business Analysts, offering clear, real-world examples of how we deliver value and drive better business outcomes.

I love the 8-step business analysis process and practical techniques, which can be adapted to any industry, domain, or project, helping teams stay aligned and focused on success.

Additionally, the book tackles the hot topic of Artificial Intelligence, showing how BAs can start leveraging AI to boost their productivity in a rapidly changing landscape. This isn't just another BA book—**it's the kind of valuable resource I wish I had earlier in my career.**

—James Dean,
Business Analyst, Mentor & President, IIBA Ireland Chapter

Laura's book, *The Value-Driven Business Analyst,* stands out by clearly and effectively highlighting the significant value Business Analysts contribute throughout the software development process.

Drawing on her deep expertise in implementing digital solutions and her experience coaching and training hundreds, if not thousands, of students through The Business Analyst Blueprint® training program, Laura offers invaluable, real-world insights.

In a dynamic industry landscape shaped by the rise of AI and increased competition, **this book is a must-have for both early-career and experienced Business Analysts committed to achieving excellence in their role.**

—Patrick Giwa, Ph.D.,
Creator AIBA Academy

When you're starting out in a business analyst career, it can be tough to know what 'high-quality' looks like without seeing how a skilled BA does their work. Laura Brandenburg's *The Value-Driven Business Analyst* fills that gap, offering practical wisdom and thoughtful framing that have made her a go-to resource for me since I began my own BA career journey.

Through success strategies, specific examples of deliverable types, and insights on leveraging AI to meet project needs, Laura equips you with ideas and inspiration to tackle your own projects.

Whether you're just getting started or looking to refine your skills, this book is more than just a great read—it's a resource you'll keep coming back to as you navigate the diverse challenges of business analysis that inevitably arise on every project. It's the kind of book you can thumb through whenever you need a fresh perspective or practical advice.

—Vanessa Grant,
Salesforce Business Analyst

THE VALUE-DRIVEN BUSINESS ANALYST

Practical Techniques
for Effective Business Analysis

LAURA BRANDENBURG

Bridging
the Gap

The Value-Driven Business Analyst: Practical Techniques
for Effective Business Analysis
By Laura Brandenburg

© 2025 Laura Brandenburg

Published by Clear Spring Business Analysis LLC
The parent company of Bridging the Gap

Bridging
the Gap

ISBN: 978-0-9838611-7-1 (softcover)
Library of Congress Cataloging in Publication Data

First Edition
Printed in the United States of America

*To all those doing business analysis, no matter your title,
industry, or location, and doing your part to make
the world a better place. This book is for you.*

Contents

Business Analyst Manifesto

Out of chaos, we create order.

Out of disagreement, we create alignment.

Out of ambiguity, we create clarity.
But most of all, we create positive change
for the organizations we serve.

Business analysts lead teams from the inside out. We create positive change for our organizations. We inspire others to follow us on our path toward positive change. We help everyone understand exactly what that change is and how they can contribute to it. We help teams discover what the change should be.

Introduction

Do you excel at creating clarity out of ambiguity, alignment out of disagreement, and order out of chaos? Do you create positive change for your organization?

Then perhaps you, like me, are a business analyst.

You may have discovered the business analysis skill set decades ago and felt like everything in your career started to make sense. Or perhaps you have just discovered the role and sense possibility. Perhaps you feel like I do, that you are in a dream role, using your full intellectual capabilities, along with your problem-solving and communication skills, to do meaningful good in the world.

If you are looking for a set of value-driven best practices to apply in a business analysis role on a software initiative that you can confidently stand behind, this book is for you. The practices in this book are distilled to their essentials and can work even in a fast-paced "do it now" environment.

If you've been looking for a set of tools and strategies to support great analysis and help you break down resistance, this is the book for you. The practices in this book will help you overcome the opposition to analysis work and fully engage stakeholders in owning and discovering value-added solutions.

International Institute of Business Analysis™ (IIBA®) defines business analysis as "the practice of enabling change in an enterprise by defining needs and recommending solutions that deliver value to stakeholders."[1] This definition is all-encompassing. I love the opportunities unleashed by such a comprehensive definition, yet find it difficult at times to make it practical and tactical. So for the

---

[1] *A Guide to the Business Analysis Body of Knowledge,* 3rd editon (IIBA, 2015), p 2.

purposes of this book, I'm going to take a more restrictive view and focus on how the practice of business analysis unfolds on software initiatives.

We'll start from being tasked with performing business analysis on an idea or concept or business problem. From there, this book traces the process of aligning all necessary business and technology stakeholders on the solution to be delivered and how that solution fits into the overall business model and flow, ending with assessing the value created by the solution. In this context, I use the term "business analyst" to refer to anyone who does business analysis activities and leverages business analysis skills, no matter their role or job title.

The Value Business Analysts Create

When you finish this book, I want you to feel so grounded in the value of business analysis that you palpably radiate confidence. I want you to feel like Kira. Initially, Kira experienced a lot of self-doubt when it came to sending out requirements-related emails. She'd struggle with knowing who to copy on an email because she didn't want to waste their time. After getting clear on the value she was creating, she worried much less about this detail, because she knew each email she was sending was important and moved the project forward. She knew she was making a difference.

There are many, many ways that business analysts create value. Here are just a few:

- You capture all requirements, which reduces rework and minimizes last-minute changes and delays.
- You identify the underlying business problem or opportunity the initiative will address and ensure that it has meaning and value to the business.

- You ensure that stakeholders agree on what they want and what's possible, and reduce friction by maintaining engagement and buy-in as decisions get made.
- You identify opportunities to do more with less, simplify solutions, and eliminate unnecessary effort by understanding the business objectives and exploring possible solution options.

Having a structured process enables you to deliver value in this way. The eight-step process covered in this book will help you:

- Thrive in fast-paced environments by choosing the right techniques at the right times and not creating documentation for its own sake.
- Cultivate credibility with a flexible yet structured approach so you can make the biggest possible impact.
- Manage expectations and articulate a complete picture of what business analysis needs to happen, so you can work strategically and intentionally to build momentum while minimizing risk.
- Cultivate consistency among business analyst team members, reducing the time you spend training stakeholders on the business analysis process and generating better outcomes, even among business analysts with mixed skill levels.

Your investment in the right level of analysis now will save you and your team mountains of work further on, and help them avoid building something the business doesn't want and perhaps will never use. This is what makes business analysis such valuable work.

My Career Journey

I'm guessing you might want to know a bit more about me and what qualifies me to mentor you through this process. I've been through a lot of what I'm guessing you are going through. There was a time that I was unclear on what business analysis is, what makes it valuable, and how to advance my career. Despite these trepidations, I started to see that no matter what industry I was in, or what type of project I was on, or even how my organization defined "project," I could find a way to make a difference with my business analysis skill set.

My title didn't matter.

The methodology didn't matter.

I started my business analyst career as a systems analyst, after building technical competence on the testing team. The first time I struggled through putting together a use case, something clicked deep inside my psyche and I just knew I'd found the meaningful work I'd been craving. And as I navigated complex conversations and problem-solving discussions with business and technical stakeholders, I felt myself leveraging my intellect in increasingly meaningful and impactful ways.

But even though I loved the work, I felt like I was in a made-up role created on the back of a dysfunctional organization. It didn't feel like a career to me—yet.

As I shifted companies, I came to realize how powerful the foundational business analysis skills were in creating more successful outcomes on all kinds of projects and in different types of organizations. What started out feeling like a jack-of-all-trades role for plugging gaps in the software development process began to feel like an essential function to drive positive business outcomes.

Eventually I found myself not-so-gently pushed into building a 15-person team of business analysts, project managers, and quality assurance engineers. I got much clearer on what value-driven business analysis looks like. Qualities such as a strategic perspective, analyzing the right thing at the right time, asking good questions, listening deeply, managing relationships, and meeting deadlines while not overlooking critical requirements set my top-performing team members apart.

Around this time I discovered that business analysis was a real profession, not just a made-up role that I happened to be good at. Some amazing professionals had formed IIBA and were developing a body of knowledge. My awareness of the role and the related skill set was now informed by important work to articulate a business analysis profession.

Yet I was riddled with self-doubt. I worked overtime out of fear, and stressed myself out trying to please everyone. One day I couldn't handle the toxic environment I suddenly found myself in. I was unprepared to set boundaries around downright unrealistic deadlines and unjust treatment of my team members, so I quit. I had no plan; just my savings. I collected myself just enough to start seeking out business analysis consulting and contracting roles, right in time for the initial wave of agile transformations. My new foundation in this profession shifted out from underneath me.

Those of you who have been around since the early 2000s will remember those dark days when all you could hear was the deafening threat of agile saying "There's no BA role here!" Those of you just joining us, let's just say that this is a traumatizing aspect of the professional history of business analysis. We're still reclaiming our role in the software development world—just in time for the next wave of transformation, reorganizing around products and value streams and the shifts enabled by generative AI.

I threw out all my tried-and-true ways in order to fit in as a contractor on agile teams and made some rookie mistakes. I embraced change that led to unnecessary rework just because "we're agile." I lost track of the big picture, and even alienated developers who were doing some business analysis work by overstepping my role. All these stories are in this book, because integrating business analysis practices with agile software development methodologies is how we create value in our modern-day world. And because I've learned just as much from my mistakes as my successes.

Around 2010, when I started to train other business analysts (albeit reluctantly at first—I am certainly not immune to the imposter syndrome that plagues so many business analysts), I started to see that the handful of business analysis techniques I use had been more effective for me than the most robust methodologies, whether from agile or business analysis circles.

While teaching, I started to see how analytical techniques like process maps, use cases, wireframes, and data models cultivate analytical thinking. Learning to analyze leads you to ask better questions. A structured approach guides you on exactly what to do next and achieve better business outcomes.

In essence, business analysis is a teachable skill set.

I began to articulate the steps I take to be effective on any type of initiative and collaborate with any sort of team. I considered all the initiatives I'd ever been part of and what made them succeed or fail. That analysis led me to the eight-step Business Analysis Process that forms the structure of this book and is the foundation of The Business Analyst Blueprint®. Today, thousands of business analysts and professionals with all kinds of titles have used this process to add more value and structure their work in a systematic, practical way. My hope is that when you've finished this book, you will too.

The Eight-Step Business Analysis Process and The Business Analyst Blueprint®

Let's start with the eight steps that underlie value-driven business analysis and collaboration with any sort of team, whether agile, product-centric, or organized around value streams.

This process is structured but lightweight, because no one, especially not a value-driven business analyst, has time for pointless documentation or analysis rabbit holes. Everything has to make an impact and move the organization forward.

While it might go without saying, documentation is not the goal of business analysis. Clarity and alignment are the goals. Helping the business stakeholders clarify what they want, ensuring their vision is complete, detailed, and represents a desired understanding of the solution, and then communicating this vision to the implementation team are the goals.

Each of the eight steps in the process is about progressing toward alignment and clarity:

1. **Get oriented.** Start actively contributing as quickly as possible by managing expectations and conducting preliminary stakeholder analysis.
2. **Discover the primary business objectives.** Ensure that the initiative solves the right business need or problem.
3. **Define scope.** Align stakeholders on the scope of the solution.
4. **Formulate your business analysis plan.** Identify the needed deliverables, work, and timeline, and decide who needs to be involved.
5. **Define the detailed requirements.** Discover, analyze, and validate the detailed requirements, ensuring that the business stakeholders feel like they own the solution.

6. **Support the technical implementation.** Partner with the technical team and ensure they have everything they need to be successful.

7. **Help the business implement the solution.** Support business stakeholders during implementation, user acceptance testing, and rollout so they ultimately get what they need.

8. **Assess the value created by the solution**. Assess the solution's return on investment (ROI), celebrate the team's accomplishments, and improve your business analysis process.

Figure 1. The Business Analysis Process

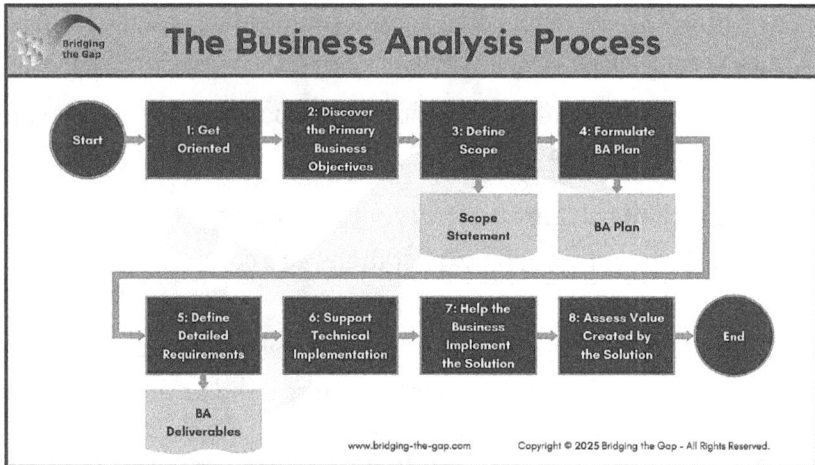

This book explores this process and ways to adjust it to work on different projects and in different organizations. It discusses how to break through resistance along the way and how to use this process as a launching point to advance a career in business analysis.

But isn't every project different?

Yes, indeed.

While you will always use your intelligence to navigate exactly how to apply a set of best practices in a given situation, there is a process you can use again and again as a business analyst. The steps in this process will be relevant regardless of your industry, your location, the project type, or even the software development methodology in place within your organization.

For a long time, I believed developing a structured approach to business analysis simply wasn't possible. That belief limited me. I've seen similar limiting beliefs in many business analysts I know. Experienced, successful analysts might feel that a process won't work or is too rigid; they have a magical ability to know what to do on a project, and others either have this ability or they don't. This mindset prevents them from effectively leading and mentoring other business analysts and establishing structures that support value-driven business analysis on initiatives across their organizations. Newer analysts who have this mindset fall into a reactive mode, often taking on lower-impact tasks than they otherwise would and focusing on the solution rather than the business problem to be solved.

Our exploration of the eight-step process will include deep dives into techniques in three high-level skill areas:

- business process analysis – how to discover, analyze, and improve business operations
- software requirements – what the software needs to functionally do to support the business
- data modeling – how the software needs to store and manage data to support the business

The techniques in these three skill areas, along with the Business Analysis Process, make up The Business Analyst Blueprint®.

Figure 2. The Business Analyst Blueprint®

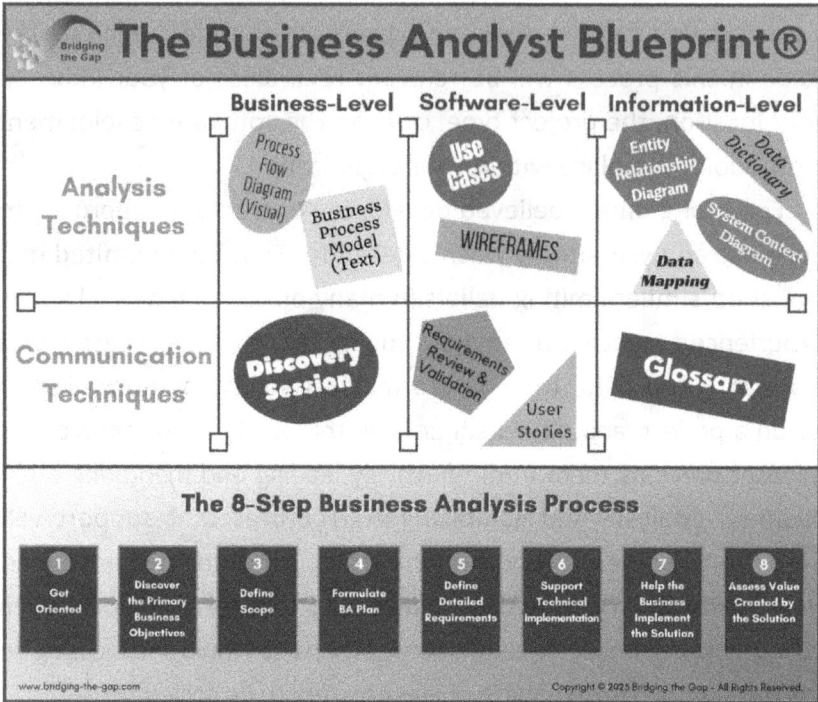

Because generative AI is creating so many opportunities for business analysts to enhance their productivity and value-creating outcomes, each chapter includes ideas for using AI to be more efficient and create more value. Always check with your organization before uploading documents or sharing any proprietary or confidential information with a generative AI tool, as many organizations have strict standards in place. Use these ideas only if organizational policies allow, and choose internal tools instead of public chatbots when available.

Download Your Success Pack

Throughout the book I refer to documents and templates that I've found invaluable in my business analysis work. I have compiled these as a free Business Analyst Success Pack available on my website at: www.bridging-the-gap.com/successpack.

The Success Pack includes the following annotated templates:

- Business Analysis Deliverables List
- Business Analysis Plan Business
- Business Analysis Skills Assessment
- Business Process Document
- Glossary
- Quick Wins Assessment
- Scope Statement
- Use Case

Because they are annotated, these templates are also useful for training AI. When you download the Success Pack, you'll also receive a free video training on how to use these templates to train an AI tool to be more effective.

The Challenges Business Analysts Face

As necessary as this work is, the business analysis role and skill set are often undervalued and unappreciated. Many business analysts find themselves in situations like these:

- rushing to meet aggressive deadlines
- being assigned after all the interesting decisions have been made to "figure out the details"
- being held to commitments made by others, only to have critical stakeholders decline meetings and ignore emails

- struggling with a lack of clarity about the role and so much resistance from team members that advocating for best practices feels impossible
- being pulled in multiple directions—tester, product manager, project manager, product owner, customer support representative, data analyst, report runner, administrative assistant, SQL administrator—in a way that feels satisfying but leaves little time for business analysis

Challenges like these can leave business analysts feeling stuck—trapped in too many roles or in too specialized an area with no clear promotion path and no clear career advancement options.

Another common challenge is hearing (or even feeling) that analysis just slows things down. Wouldn't it be faster to just have the developers talk to the business users and build what they say they want? In the short term, perhaps. It certainly feels faster to skip right to Step 5, dive into defining detailed requirements, and start coding some solution options! But then you get to Step 7, implementing the solution, and the business submits dozens of poorly documented change requests and everyone gets bogged down in finger-pointing and frustration.

And far too often, business analysts get in their own way, letting perfectionism get in the way of collaboration by trying to get things too perfect too early. This does slow things down, and it's a habit to break ASAP. This book will help.

Some business analysts are too technology focused, or too business focused, and lose the balance that keeps them objective and solution focused.

- A business analyst that's too technology focused tends to concentrate on the software aspect of the solution and tries to train the business to speak in technical jargon, which leads to misunderstandings and an incomplete view of the problem being solved.

- A business analyst that's too business focused tends to get too absorbed in the business problem, lets scope run wild, and may map out a lot of processes without being clear about what the software actually needs to do to support the business.

This process is all about finding the sweet spot and leveraging best practices to unite business and technical perspectives so that meaningful work gets done and actual business problems get solved.

Despite all these challenges, good business analysis practices can be a grounding force during business and technology transformations. Organizations are starting to notice that hiring more software developers does not get them the bottom-line business results they need. And while AI tools can write a lot of code and documentation, they can't yet get stakeholders from across the business on the same page about the outcome, choose the right techniques at the right times, facilitate structured conversations, or do the type of analytical thinking and exploration needed to solve problems specific to your organization. What's more, to leverage AI intelligently to craft models and draft documentation, you need the foundational skills to evaluate the output and the know-how to craft prompts.[2]

This brings me to one of my favorite mantras:

On every successful project, you'll find a business analyst.

---

[2] Angela Wick and Tim Coventry, *Futureproof: Amplifying Agility with AI and Insightful Business Analysis* (IIBA, 2024), p. 99.

They may not have the title. They may not even be aware that they are doing business analysis. But someone is ensuring that the right problem is solved, that everyone understands the problem and solution in detail, and that all key stakeholders agree about what the software is going to do and why.

Getting the Most out of This Book

Technique by technique, step-by-step, this book explains the Business Analysis Process and associated techniques from The Business Analyst Blueprint®. With this flexible set of best practices, you can strengthen your credibility by ensuring that your role and your team deliver real value to the business.

Where you are in your career may affect how you want to approach this book:

- Aspiring business analysts should use this material to better understand the role, anticipate the challenges they may face, and identify skills and experiences that may transfer to a business analyst career.[3]

- Newer business analysts can refer to this book as a go-to resource and a guide to navigating the role with authority of an experienced business analyst, keeping in mind the processes and practices in place within the organization. This book supplies copious amounts of techniques to employ, questions to ask, and expectations to set that will help you undertake your first projects more successfully.

- Experienced business analysts may be aware of much of the material in this book, but can still benefit from ideas and suggestions for adjusting work, improving practices, and more fully articulating the value that business analysis

---

[3] My first book, *How to Start a Business Analyst Career,* is a step-by-step guide to making the career transition to business analysis.

creates. Approach this book with a beginner's mind, as there could be many practices you are aware of but aren't applying day-to-day. Going from awareness to application could be the shift that helps your career take off.

- Business analyst leaders can use this book to develop or improve the framework the team uses on their projects. It may also cultivate awareness of the techniques and practices that have made you successful, so you are better prepared to mentor and guide the newer business analysts on your team.

No matter where you are in your career, explore the final chapter on career paths within and beyond business analysis for ideas on how to leverage all the value-creating work you do as a business analyst to advance your career and reach your full potential.

Business analysts that read together, grow together. A great way to go deeper with the material is to start a book club with your business analyst team, your local connections, or even a virtual group of other business analysts who share your industry, business domain, or career goals.

Thank You for Being a Business Analyst

I'm so glad you are on this journey. I firmly believe that business analysts make the world a better place. They break down barriers to collaboration and help ensure that the people who build things build what matters. There are so many huge problems to solve in this world, and while you might feel like whatever bit of software you are working on is inconsequential in the big picture, believe me, it's not. Your work matters. Your contribution matters.

Just today I called my dentist with new dental insurance. Looking up my plan and submitting my claim took them five minutes. I'm grateful to the business analyst who designed a system that was so easy to use, especially since this is not my typical experience with insurance-related systems. And because the call took five minutes instead of 20, I got to start writing this book, which I hope will have a profound impact on you and your career.

This is just one system out of dozens, perhaps hundreds, that I've directly used or indirectly benefited from today—systems that enhance my life and expand my potential.

Yes, the world needs more business analysts, and we need you to be at your best.

I don't need to remind you of the big problems we need to solve, from climate change to our food system to social unrest to all too much violence. There are a lot. Whether you are working on them directly or supporting those who do by making sure their insurance pays for their dental checkup, thank you.

⏩ Next Steps

Each chapter closes with a set of actions you can take to apply what you've learned and advance your skill set, projects, and career. Before moving ahead, here are three steps you can take to prepare for this journey:

- Consider the eight steps in the Business Analysis Process. Which ones are part of your work today? Which represent opportunities to expand your role and impact?
- Take a moment to dream about what being a value-driven business analyst means to you. What's truly in it for you to master this skill set while helping others appreciate the value you bring to a project?

- Download your bonus templates and resources at: www.bridging-the-gap.com/successpack so you have them at hand as you read.

Once you have your Success Pack, it's time for Step 1, "Get Oriented," because before we can define the business objectives for your project, we need a little context and background. Let's get started.

1

Get Oriented

Business analysts often face pressure to contribute almost immediately when joining a project team. Sometimes the initiative is
already underway; other times there are vague notions about what
the initiative is or why it exists. Ambiguity is common, and it's the
business analyst's job to clarify the business objectives, scope, and
requirements as quickly as possible.

But that doesn't mean that it makes sense to get knee-deep
into the detailed requirements right away. Taking some time to
get oriented—a few hours, a few days, or at most a few weeks—
will **ensure the project moves quickly and in the right direction.**
Intentionally moving slowly in the beginning helps the team move
much, much faster (and more effectively) later.

This theme will resurface again and again (and again) throughout
this book. Teams often move faster in the long term when they pause
in the short term to get really clear. It may feel like slowing things
down, but it actually speeds things up. Not all movement is movement
in the right direction.

One of the ways business analysts create tremendous value is by
ensuring that software development effort focuses on meaningful
outcomes for the business. Applying this mindset to our own
work ensures we're making a valuable contribution. Step 1 is about
establishing enough of a foundation to keep the team from wasting
time and energy going in the wrong direction.

This chapter discusses how to clarify your role, determine the primary stakeholders, understand the project history, and understand the existing systems and businesses process. With this foundation, you can start collaborating with the key business stakeholders to understand the business objectives—why this project is important.

Step 1 is critical, but don't overinvest or get stuck here. For most initiatives, a few days will be more than enough. Some will only need a few hours of research and conversation. A few rare cases, such as a major system upgrade, could require a few weeks or even a few months understanding the existing systems and business processes, but even that work will be focused on providing useful material for the rest of the steps.

Defining a Project

In this book, the term "project" refers to a one-time set of activities meant to implement a change in the organization and achieve a particular goal. The change could occur in the context of a product, a value stream, or a portfolio. Once a project is complete, consistent process implementation sustains the changes. Other ways of describing work include initiatives, enhancements, requests, changes, or backlogs.

In an agile context, a business analyst may focus on a set of backlog items the team is focused on over the next 3–6 months to optimize a value stream or business area. In a product-centric organization, the focus could be on a set of initiatives or enhancement requests. A "project" could also be a maintenance request, a new report, or a so-called tweak to an existing system.

Any request, even one that only takes a few days or hours to implement, will benefit from analysis using this process. No matter the methodology in place or the way teams are organized, business analysts make software work *for the business.* That's what value-driven business analysis is all about.

To keep things fluid and honor the fact that business analysts contribute to many different containers of work, I use project, initiative, and change effort interchangeably throughout this book.

Clarify Your Role

One of the biggest mistakes business analysts make in new organizations or on new teams is assuming what their role will be.

There is so much inconsistency between roles from one organization and team to another. Making assumptions, even with the best of intentions, risks alienating team members, stepping on toes, and damaging your credibility. Clarifying the role avoids this. But be strategic about it, to avoid creating skepticism or undermining confidence in you.

It helps to understand a typical business analyst role. On a software project, a business analyst usually has several responsibilities:

- clarifying the business problem to be solved and ensuring the business stakeholders are aligned on the business objectives for the project
- facilitating collaboration among business and technology stakeholders about the solution and project scope
- discovering, analyzing, and validating the details of the current-state and future-state business processes, software requirements, and data requirements
- supporting the business and technology teams as they implement the solution
- measuring the project's success

I captured the essence of this role in the BA Manifesto that I wrote back in 2009:

> ### *Out of chaos, we create order.*
>
> ### *Out of disagreement, we create alignment.*
>
> ### *Out of ambiguity, we create clarity.*
>
> ### *But most of all, we create positive change for the organizations we serve.*
>
> **Business analysts lead teams from the inside out. We create positive change for our organizations. We inspire others to follow us on our path toward positive change. We help everyone understand exactly what that change is and how they can contribute to it. We help teams discover what the change should be.**

However (and this is important), not all business analyst roles are the same. Here are some of the more common variations:

- **Requirements analyzer** – The business analyst is assigned after the business objectives and scope have been defined, or there is little support for taking the time to clarify the business objectives. These business analysts are told to start by analyzing the detailed requirements.
- **Superuser** – The business analyst is in a consulting role on a software-as-a-service (SaaS) application. They support the existing application as a superuser by creating reports, administering the system, and even configuring the system using "no code" solutions. This role involves some analysis, typically of individual features, to respond to new requests.

- **Product manager/owner** – The business analyst is in a product manager or product owner role and has more responsibility and ownership when it comes to defining the business objectives and scope, versus facilitating the discovery and agreement on those items with key business stakeholders.
- **Product manager/owner support** – The business analyst is supporting a product manager or product owner who may also share some analysis responsibilities. The product owner might be responsible for defining business objectives and scope for each product enhancement while the business analyst is responsible for understanding the detailed requirements, assessing impacts, and helping the implementation team manage change.
- **Hybrid role** – The business analyst is responsible for some or all of the business analysis work as well as work from a related function such as project management, quality assurance, data analysis, or technical design.
- **Tester** – In some extreme cases, the business analyst is assigned in the testing phase, often with little documentation and few requirements in place, and so must both figure out the intended scope and test the functionality of the system.

The type of initiative can also shape the business analyst role in interesting ways.

- **Custom software,** where the team is coding functionality from scratch, requires more detailed and specific software and data requirements.
- **Off-the-shelf solutions,** where the team is licensing software or accessing existing software in the cloud, often to replace

a pre-existing system or set of manual processes and spreadsheets, require more focus on business process and data migration and less on detailed software requirements, unless the team is customizing or configuring the system.

- **System integrations,** where the team is getting two separate systems to "talk" to one another, require in-depth data modeling and data mapping requirements.
- **Upgrading legacy systems** to a new version of the same system requires a strong focus on data and user migration, onboarding users to the new system, and decommissioning the old system.
- **Ongoing maintenance** typically requires evaluating each request or issue to understand the business problem and detailed requirements to address it.

So how do you clarify your role?

The obvious place to start is with the job description, if it exists. How does it describe the role? What techniques are mentioned? What's the overall goal for the business analyst?

But even with a job description in hand, you want to clarify expectations, every single time. Here's how that conversation could go with your manager, the primary sponsor, or the project manager.

I'm excited about this project and can't wait to start. Before I do, I want to be sure we're on the same page about what you want me to accomplish. My understanding is that I will be identifying stakeholders to understand their current-state business processes, identifying features for the new solution we're implementing, and then collaborating with the third-party vendor to ensure they have everything they need to successfully configure the solution. That will mean analyzing the software or functional requirements,

*defining future-state business processes, and docu-
menting any data migration and business rules. Is this
your understanding as well?*

If you get a positive response:

*Great. My first step is to identify the primary
stakeholders. I know Bob from Accounting is a key
stakeholder, and I imagine we need someone from
Sales and Marketing as well. Do you know who those
people might be or should I start with Bob and work
out from there?*

If you get a negative response:

*OK, well this is a great time to clear up expectations.
What do you expect of me?*

Or, you could pressure test each aspect of the role.

*I feel that analyzing the current-state business
processes would be important to ensure we don't
overlook any high-priority features. Would you agree?*
        *And then we'll want to look at the functionality of
the current system and determine what configurations
and customizations we require, right? {Here you may
discover an assumption that there will be no customizations—an important reference point on scope.}*
        *And I imagine we will be bringing over our current
data, and we'll want to be sure this mapping meets
the business needs, right? {Here you could discover
that someone else owns data migration. Add that
person to your stakeholder list and build a relationship
with them as the project unfolds.}*

This will get help you get started. As you meet with stakehold-ers, share these expectations and ask more questions:

- Have you worked with a business analyst before? What was great about working with them?
- Here is what I plan to deliver. Is there anything else you expect from me?
- Do you have any questions or concerns about my approach?

Now, you could get an entirely different response:

Actually, that's not why we hired you at all. We did all that months ago and the system is about go live. We need you to work with the business to develop UAT (user acceptance testing) scripts and make sure this thing works.

This person is essentially asking you to jump right to Step 7 and trust the business analysis work that's been done (or not). You get to choose how to handle the situation. Often, it makes sense to meet the team where they are and contribute as best you can. Review available documentation and ask a lot of questions. Set yourself up to get involved earlier on the next initiative.

If you don't have much background on your role, these questions can provide clarity:

- What's the business analyst's primary goal?
- What methodology or software development frameworks are in place for this team?
- What inputs will I receive before I start work?
- What deliverables is the business analyst responsible for creating for this team? Do you have an example for me to review?

- Who reviews and receives each of these deliverables? What's the next step they take as a result of receiving completed deliverables?
- What meetings does a business analyst typically schedule throughout the lifecycle of an initiative?
- Are there any standing meetings I'm expected to attend or facilitate?
- What tools does the business analyst use?

It's also a great idea to have a set of templates or deliverables to use as a starting point. The downloadable resources in this book are a great place to start. Just be sure to confirm that stakeholders are expecting the same type of deliverable—many terms have different meanings in different organizations, and even within the same organization.

Here's what's important: Just because you did things one way on one team doesn't mean that will work universally. Collaboration and flexibility are key. This is true even across teams that use similar methodologies. On my second agile team, I made the mistake of assuming that the approach I had used successfully on my first team would work just as well. Things went sideways fast when I started reviewing wireframes with a developer who was also the user interface designer and who felt I was overstepping.

If it sounds like I'm going a bit overboard while cautioning you to clarify expectations, it's because I know firsthand the challenges that surface when you don't! Clarifying expectations gets you on the fast track to adding the right kind of value, and prevents unnecessary tasks, redundant work, and wasted effort.

A good practice is to meet with each person in an adjacent role to clarify shared expectations, communication needs, responsibilities, and how you can best collaborate. Key roles to reach out to include the project manager, product owner and/or product manager, technical lead, and any other analysts (systems analysts, technical analysts, process analysts).

Determine Your Primary Stakeholders

Next, identify the primary stakeholders to engage in defining the business objectives and scope, as well as any subject matter experts to consult early in the initiative. Start with a few key stakeholders who have critical input and authority to approve the scope.

There two key stakeholders to identify:

- **Who is funding the initiative?** This person is the primary sponsor and makes the final decisions on scope, budget, and changes.
- **Who do you ultimately report to?** This person is your functional manager.

Ideally there will be only one person in each role, but the same person may fill both roles.

One of the most common questions I hear is about how to handle disagreements over business objectives and scope. When we trace this challenge to its root cause, it almost always turns out that the business analyst is stuck between multiple senior-level stakeholders with different agendas, trying to define a scope that appeases everyone. On the one hand, this is a reality of a more decentralized organization, and top-down decision-making does not always yield the best outcome. We all want to include multiple perspectives, foster collaboration, and increase creativity. On the other hand, lack of clear decisions can stall an initiative. It's in your best interest to identify the single person that can make a clear decision if all your efforts to reach a collaborative, consensus-based decision fail.

To find this person, find out who controls funding or "signs the checks." This is the sponsor. Sometimes the true sponsor is the line manager of the multiple stakeholders initially identified as sponsors, or simply an influential senior-level executive. Sometimes a product owner or product manager is the primary decision-maker but needs approval from their manager or a higher-level stake-holder on decisions affecting other areas of the business. It's best to understand how these decisions get made.

As the initiative progresses, keep the sponsor informed of key decisions even if they are not actively included in meetings and discussion. You never know when you'll need to go to them for a decision, so foster this relationship from the beginning.

Still, it is critical to foster collaboration before leaning on leader-ship for a decision. One business analyst I was coaching felt caught between the quality control and manufacturing departments in his company. The quality control team was driving the change and had clear leadership, but the change required a significant effort and retooling of the manufacturing process. Leadership within manu-facturing was resisting the change, to the point of not showing up for meetings and not providing input.

This business analyst saw a potential solution that wouldn't be as difficult for manufacturing to implement, but he couldn't get them engaged enough to even consider the option. However, he did have one ally within the manufacturing team, someone who was newer and had little seniority or decision-making power, but who could provide critical input to validate the business analyst's idea.

We talked about whether and when he could and should raise this issue with senior leadership as a risk. He knew from experience that raising a flag on manufacturing would create a lot of negative energy and damage the relationships he'd worked so hard to build. But if he didn't raise this issue, the accountability for the delay and lack of consensus might ultimately fall to him. This is a real dilemma that business analysts often confront.

We ultimately agreed that he should start by working with his ally to get his idea in front of the manufacturing leaders. If that didn't work, he would notify the manufacturing leaders before raising the issue more publicly, so at least they would have every opportunity to engage and couldn't feel blindsided.

During our next session, he celebrated that this strategy worked. He never had to escalate, because once the manufacturing leaders saw how the changes could unfold they bought into the outcomes.

This example highlights the tension business analysts often face. In an ideal world there will be a single sponsor who makes the important decisions and breaks gridlock, but reality is much more nuanced and complex. Even if there is a clear sponsor, that doesn't mean we should escalate every requirements issue. It wastes their time, it doesn't create a positive team environment, and it certainly won't enhance your credibility as a business analyst. So yes, know who the ultimate sponsor is, but take care about when and how you leverage their decision-making power.

In addition to the sponsor and your manager, there are other stakeholders who can help you get oriented quickly:

- **subject matter experts** who understand the current-state business processes and are willing to share information
- **technical experts** who understand the technology systems and are willing to share information
- **the project manager** (titled or otherwise) who is responsible for managing the project

It's helpful to keep a list of key stakeholders, as shown in figure 3.

Figure 3. A sample stakeholder list

Stakeholder Name	Job Title	Role on Project	Communication Preferences
Malik Johnson	Chief Operations Officer	Executive Sponsor	Weekly status emails, monthly calls
Priya Sharma	IT Project Manager	Project Manager	Daily stand-ups, Daily stand-ups, project dashboard
Alex Morgan	Business Analyst	Business Analyst	Collaborative work shops, Slack messages
Taylor Nguyen	Software Architect	Solution Design Lead	Technical design documents, email summaries
Jordan Walker	Change Management Specialists	Change Management Lead	Weekly meetings, video updates

Stakeholders are the lifeblood of your project. They will provide critical information each step of the way and make the decisions that move the change effort forward, or they will withhold critical information and procrastinate on decisions, thereby delaying it.

It's never too early for a business analyst to invest in building relationships and open communication channels with stakeholders. A successful initiative requires a strong network of internal and sometimes external stakeholders engaged in a coordinated and collaborative effort. Your contributions are essential to getting and keeping everyone on track.

Understand the History

No one wants to repeat work that's already done or rehash previously made decisions. Understanding the history of the initiative can provide critical information about the state of the effort and where early contributions can make the greatest impact.

Even a new initiative probably has some history. When a manager dashes off a quick email about a new project, it's often because a problem was discussed in an executive meeting and that manager now owns the issue. Before that executive discussion, the person who raised the issue probably had discussions within their department or in other settings. Those discussions are part of the project's history.

Other times, a business analyst is brought in toward the middle of the project. Ideally, the business analyst would be one of the first people assigned to the project, but that's not always the case. It's not uncommon to join a team and find that vendors have already been interviewed, or even selected, and key decisions have been made. This can be frustrating, but it's usually best to start contributing rather than complaining. Once people see your value, it's easier to get assigned to the next initiative earlier so you can make an even bigger impact. Look for documentation to review or email chains to read, and have detailed conversations with stakeholders about what they expect and what's happened so far. Here are some questions to ask:

- What has been discussed so far?
- Who has been involved in those discussions?
- What documentation exists?
- What decisions have been made?
- What are the primary objectives?
- Who needs to be involved?

Clarify what's been discussed, what's been decided, and what's been communicated. Stakeholders may present their opinion as a decision or misinterpret that a decision has been made when it hasn't. A business stakeholder may recall clearly communicating their requirements to a technical stakeholder who believes they are waiting for more clarity. Asking multiple stakeholders about the same decisions can uncover conflicts and provide insight about where you can contribute by facilitating discussions that lead to decisions that are clearly communicated to the right people.

Verify every decision with key stakeholders and capture discussions so they can be communicated to everyone who might need to know to be effective in their role. Also recognize that intended outcomes could shift and decisions could change as you work through the process.

Understand Existing Systems and Processes

Most often, new projects replace or improve existing processes and systems:

- a new software system replaces a manual process managed via emails and spreadsheets
- a new software system replaces all or part of an existing technology system
- an existing process needs to be replaced by an improved process

In some organizations, you'll find comprehensive, up-to-date information that contains current system requirements and current-state (also called "as is") business processes. More often, current-state documentation will be incomplete and out of date. When documentation does exist, honor your stakeholders' time by reviewing it before asking questions. A good first question to ask is whether there are any documents that will help you get up to speed.

After reviewing available documentation, here are some ways to confirm current-state business processes and system capabilities:

- Ask for a demonstration of an existing system by a subject matter expert.

- Observe a subject matter expert as they perform their day job, with permission to ask questions as they work.
- Request a technical overview of the system from a technical expert. Software developers are the obvious choice, but testers and technical writers can provide valuable overviews and may be better at explaining technical concepts in business-friendly terms.
- Ask follow-up questions based on the documentation.
- Request access to the system(s) and explore the functionality independently.

The goal is getting a high-level understanding of the current process and systems. It's common to have information overload at this stage, so consider organizing the information in folders or a digital notebook. Turning unstructured notes into first-pass models, even if they are loose and annotated with questions and gaps, will provide structure that speeds understanding.

Consider producing the following deliverables early in the initiative:

- A high-level overview of the business process in a process map format with a list of the key business processes to analyze in future steps, possibly on a virtual white board with sticky notes. This deliverable is covered in more detail under "Technique in Focus" in chapter 2.
- A list of existing systems and their current capabilities, potentially in the form of a system context diagram, which is described in "Technique in Focus" in chapter 3.
- A glossary of key terminology, acronyms, and definitions as described under "Technique in Focus" later in this chapter. It's also helpful to note inconsistencies in terminology usage between stakeholder groups and supporting documents.

- A collection of process-related assets such as spreadsheets, templates, screenshots, and work aids used by those who complete the process today. These will be analyzed in more detail in later steps.

The idea here is to go broad, not deep. Learn just enough to ask intelligent questions about the business objectives, which requires a basic understanding of the current environment and the context being changed. You'll iterate on and deepen this analysis during the initiative. For example, defining scope might prompt a deeper exploration of current system capabilities to determine whether they could provide the needed functionality. Defining detailed requirements may require even more in-depth exploration in the context of detailed future-state business processes and business rules.

While I'm not one to engage in many theoretical debates when it comes to business analysis, I've found that my advice to focus on the current state before the future state can cause a lot of spirited discussion. Many practitioners wholeheartedly agree. Others make a strong case for starting with the intended future state, investing energy in what you want to create, not what exists today.

Defining the future state is critical—this is what business analysis and the requirements process is all about! But we also want to be sure we're not limited by our current assumptions. Taking time to analyze and understand the current state should never create limitations.

However, as a business analyst approaching new stakeholders on a new project, you need to meet people where they're at, and that's their current state—problems, issues, and all. What's more, starting with the future state makes it easy to overlook nuances and exceptions. These exceptions don't just fade away because they weren't included in the up-front analysis. They tend to surface when the business stakeholders start conducting user acceptance tests, when these requirements are much more costly to implement and often cause significant delays.

Finally, it can be easy for stakeholders to get excited about the future state, particularly when they see a demo of a new software tool that looks and feels much more modern than what they have today. This is why so many initiatives start with stakeholders focused on a solution and not a problem to be solved, an issue we'll address in more depth in the next chapter. Being grounded in but not limited by the current state encourages disciplined thinking when evaluating new tools and opportunities. It allows analysts to ask the hard but insightful questions that can sway the course of the entire change effort and ultimately make it more successful.

Enhance Your Productivity with Generative AI

- Describe the initiative and other participants, then ask for suggestions about how the business analyst role can make the most impact.
- Upload background documents and ask for a summary and next steps.
- Upload recordings of demos and observations and request drafts of process and system documentation.
- Use AI to start a glossary of key terms.

✔ Success Strategy: Handling Overwhelm

For the first step in an eight-step process, this might feel like a lot! A bit of overwhelm is normal and natural. Early business analysis means taking in a lot of information (much of it conflicting), meeting new people, and orienting to a new team. Overwhelm is a good sign of receiving the information needed to structure the change effort and drive next steps.

The risk is in allowing overwhelm to consume us and stall work, convincing us that we need to know, discover, and analyze everything before moving forward. This is one of the quickest ways to lose credibility. Inability to break through the overwhelm will keep you stuck on smaller initiatives and on smaller tasks within projects.

So here's one of my most powerful success tips. To move through overwhelm, focus on the very next decision:

- What vendor will we choose for implementation?
- Who needs to be involved?
- How do we get this initiative approved?
- Which off-the-shelf product will we choose?
- Which systems do we need to integrate?
- Which business objectives are critical?

Out of all the possibilities, choose the one decision your team needs to make to move the initiative forward and build momentum. You may determine this by considering the project implementation process or something the sponsor says. Once you choose it, focus on that decision. It will clarify which details are important now and which can be safely set aside for later.

For example, choosing a vendor generally means knowing which product you will implement. Choosing a product requires clarity on your business objectives. You can enhance your credibility and gain buy-in for business analysis work by presenting your analysis as the next step to get where your sponsor wants to go.

To help us choose an appropriate off-the-shelf product,
I'll understand our current-state business processes
and what gaps we have in our current system, so we
can choose a product that better meets our needs.

> *To help us get this project approved, I'll understand each key stakeholders' perspective of what's most important and gain alignment and clarity on the potential scope.*

It might feel like you have to make all the decisions right now, but that's impossible and will keep you stuck. Focus on the bigger decisions that influence the rest of the initiative first, and then move on to more detailed decisions will create clarity and build momentum.

Another way to frame this success tip is to defer whatever decisions you can. You can think of this as waiting until the last responsible moment to make a decision, a concept introduced by Mary and Tom Poppendieck.[4] In this view, delaying decisions allows for gathering as much relevant information as possible in order to make better-informed decisions, avoiding patterns of premature commitments that might lead to unnecessary constraints or waste.

While trying to make all the decisions up front bogs you down, a pattern of making intentional decisions builds momentum. This is the essence of business analysis: a relentless focus on one good decision after another to create value for the business. Identify the one next decision and focus on that to mitigate the natural overwhelm.

◆》 Technique in Focus: Glossaries

Using a glossary is a fundamental technique that shortens ramp-up time and reduces information overload on a new project.

Part of the burden at this stage comes from the language in use, or the terminology itself. Different stakeholders often use the same terms to talk about different concepts, or different terms to refer

---

[4] Mary Poppendieck and Tom Poppendieck, *Lean Software Development: An Agile Toolkit* (Addison-Wesley, 2010).

to the same basic concept. This can make it seem like stakeholders disagree when they are simply talking about the same ideas using different terms!

Building a glossary is a great way to start to bring order to the chaos of inconsistent terminology. It also helps stakeholders understand each other better, and paves the way for improved relationships and collaboration. What's more, it can take you from being the least knowledgeable person in the room when it comes to the business domain to being the most savvy about the business concepts. That's a powerful and confidence-building position to be in.

A glossary is a list of terms with identifying information about each of those terms. In practice, developing a glossary is an iterative process that happens in the context of an initiative, document, or a job role. Ideally, a glossary is a living file, adjusted as new terms are discovered and the business language changes over time.

Figure 4. A business glossary

Term	Definition	Aliases	Related Terms
Applicant	A person who has submitted an *application* to indicate their interest in being considered for an open *job posting*.	Job Applicant; Candidate	
Application	A collection of information submitted by an *applicant* to a specific *job posting*.		
Candidate	See *Applicant*.		
Hiring Manager	A person employed by a hiring organization who is responsible for making the final hiring decision for an open job position.		Recruiter

---

A typical glossary includes important information about key terms used in the business. Download a glossary template as part of the Business Analyst Success Pack here: www.bridging-the-gap.com/successpack.

This template includes four elements:

- **Term** – The word or short phrase most commonly used to refer to a specific business concept
- **Definition** – A sentence or more that uniquely describes the meaning of the term
- **Alias** – Terms that used as synonyms for the primary term, including acronyms
- **Related Terms** – Terms that are different from but related to the primary term

While wading through the project information, watch for terms that show up repeatedly or in domain-specific contexts. You'll discover these terms in documents, during discussions with stakeholders, on user interface screens, on forms and templates.

You can always start with a simple document like the table shown in figure 4. Typically, as the work gains traction, you'll want to convert the glossary into a shareable electronic format, like a wiki page or a database, so it can be used by other teams and the business at large, or even referenced by an internal AI tool, which can help you use the terminology consistently in your documentation. But that's for later. The goal right now is to create a tool you can use to manage terminology related to your work.

⏩ Next Steps

Are you surprised how much there is to do before you jump in and start working on deliverables? Business analysts excel with context, and Step 1 is all about uncovering the context you need to be successful.

Value-driven business analysis is about creating order out of chaos, alignment out of disagreement, and clarity out of ambiguity. You facilitate discussions that lead to decisions that are clearly communicated to the right people. Here are some next steps to implement what you've learned:

- Clarify how your organization defines an initiative. Is it a value stream, a set of backlog items over a specific time span, or a more traditional project as part of a portfolio? It may even be an enhancement or maintenance request. Use this context as you explore each of the eight steps and the supporting techniques.
- Clarify your role and deliverables so you can make the contribution you are expected to make, gaining credibility for yourself on this team and for the business analyst role in your organization.
- Identify your primary stakeholders and start building relationships with them. Know who to ask about different topics or decisions, identify the ultimate sponsor who makes any final decisions, and know who your functional manager is.
- Understand the project history so you can avoid duplicating effort and rehashing previously made decisions, which slows down the project and damages your credibility with stakeholders.

- Understand the existing systems and processes to create a shared understanding of the starting point, so you can ask better questions and find the path forward.
- Identify the next decision that must be made to build momentum. Focus on this decision to alleviate overwhelm for you and your team.
- Draft a glossary to clarify terminology and resolve unnecessary conflicts that surface from ambiguous language use.

In this step, your work is learning what you don't know so you can be as effective and efficient as possible in the work to come. Focus on getting enough context to be effective. You won't be an expert yet, and that's OK! Learn just enough to speak intelligently and ask good questions. You can always do more research after the business objectives and scope become clear.

2

Discover the Primary Business Objectives

Now that you have some context for your new project it's time to discover, and perhaps even more importantly gain alignment from stakeholders on, the primary business objectives:

- What does value mean to the business in the context of this initiative?
- What results are you trying to create?
- What problem are you trying to solve?
- What is the potential ROI?

These are all ways of thinking about the business objectives, or outcomes to be created by the initiative.

Teams commonly jump right into defining the scope, but this can lead to unnecessary headaches. **The quickest path forward is uncovering and agreeing on the business objectives before defining scope.** It may feel slower, but it prevents significant issues that can bring the work to a screeching halt, such as detailed requirements churn while stakeholders advocate for solutions to different problems, or implementation of a solution that the business rejects or can't use.

Furthermore, clarifying the business objectives often reduces the scope of an initiative, allowing the organization to invest less to generate more value.

Consider a business sponsor who wants to introduce a new product in order to grow the company's customer base and increase revenue. Perhaps the customer service manager can't imagine servicing more customers or product configurations without implementing specific efficiencies. The marketing team believes that a new product is unnecessary because they can grow the customer base using a certain marketing strategy. The technology team sees the initiative as an opportunity to upgrade the entire system to a new platform. Business analysts who start defining scope based on these shaky foundations will be pulled in multiple directions. If you plow into the detailed requirements, you'll be stuck between many competing requests and ideas.

Even on a small change or a seemingly minor enhancement request, clarifying business objectives will make the best use of resources by ensuring that the right requirements get discovered and implemented.

Stakeholders may resist this discussion. It's possible no one has ever asked them to clarify the why behind what they want. Investing time in this step will likely bring a new best practice to the team and the organization.

Other times, the objectives are part of the business case or other high-level document used to get approval before involving the business analyst. The stakeholders may resist revisiting or rewriting these objectives, even if they aren't completely clear and actionable, because they need to maintain forward momentum. Business analysts in this situation can still ask lots of questions, clarify their own understanding, and improve the outcomes as a result.

As you navigate these discussions and gain clarity on the business objectives, team members will become more engaged and more focused on valuable outcomes. You'll cultivate loyalty and respect by demonstrating your capacity to clarify and understand what matters to them and to the business.

And I simply can't stress this enough: The clearer you get now, the easier the rest of the initiative will be!

Define Effective Business Objectives

A business objective defines the impact that the solution or change should have on the business environment. It is a target or metric that a person or organization seeks in order to make progress toward a goal. Effective business objectives are actionable, clear, and outcome oriented. The goal is for all key business stakeholders to share an understanding of two to five interrelated business objectives that the initiative will address.

But first, you need to know where you are headed and how to adjust your approach to business objectives based organizational practices.

Decide Where to Document the Business Objectives

Your organization may call business objectives something different: business requirements, business needs, business value, desired out-comes, ROI, or even key performance indicators. The name doesn't matter. It's much easier to lean into the terminology that's already in place rather than to try to shift it, particularly if you experience resistance to considering outcome-based objectives.

Business objectives can be included in any number of documents. Common candidates include scope statements, business cases, or project charters. On an agile team, business objectives could be included in an epic or other high-level document that articulates the overarching goal of the next several sprints.

Evaluate documents created early in the initiative: Do any already have a section for business objectives? Would it make sense to add a section? A senior analyst on one team I worked with had the great idea of adding a section on business objectives to the project manager's existing project plan template. It was much easier to raise visibility for the business objectives in a familiar document than to create a new one.

If the business objectives are hidden in a rarely referenced document, consider ways to make them more visible. If the original objectives are unclear and key stakeholders resist changing them, include them as is but add clarifying detail or context based on your follow-up discussions.

It doesn't matter where the business objectives are documented as long as they are actionable, clear, and outcome-focused.

Make the Business Objectives Actionable

Actionable business objectives are specific to this initiative and eliminate many possible solutions, guiding your team toward the best possible solution given the constraints and assumptions. To test whether a business objective is actionable, consider whether you could facilitate a brainstorming session to elicit specific solution ideas to meet the objective. If you could, would the team have the information they need to select the best or most appropriate ideas at the end of the brainstorming session? If your business objectives would not provide this sort of guidance, keep refining until they are fully actionable.

For example, an organization could have a goal of increasing revenue by 30% this year. No one initiative will meet this goal; it will require a collection of connected efforts and improvements. A specific change effort may have an objective of increasing the number of new customers by 10% by making the sales process more efficient so each salesperson can close more sales. This organization might choose the following business objectives:

Increase the number of new customers each month by 10% compared to the previous year's baseline.

Reduce the number of hours required for a salesperson to close a new customer by 10 hours.

In this example, the first objective doesn't stand on its own because the possibilities for increasing the number of new customers each month by 10% are virtually endless: new marketing strategies, expanded sales staff, new markets, new sales territories. By itself, the second objective wouldn't make it clear why it's important to reduce the number of hours a salesperson spends closing a new customer. Together, these objectives provide focus and clarity, and are therefore actionable.

Ensure that the business objectives fit together logically and give the team enough clarity to begin discussing scope. In this case, it seems possible that by making the sales process more efficient, the organization will be able to increase the number of new customers, which means the objectives fit together logically.

Make the Business Objectives Clear

Business objectives that are clear are unambiguous, easily understood by all stakeholders, specific, and often measurable. To be specific, an objective must address only one aspect of the business needs and paint a clear picture of the desired outcome. A lot of business objectives seem specific on the surface, but don't give you much to go on once you dig in.

One common nonspecific objective is "efficiency." It's easy to get caught by this one. Case in point: When leaving a conference in Las Vegas, I jumped into a cab to the airport and the driver asked me which way I'd like to go. I was feeling very analytical, and maybe a little sassy, having just spent a few days alongside hundreds of business analysts. I also didn't know my options. I said I wanted to take "the most efficient way."

There was a pause. Then the cab driver said, "The street is the cheapest. The highway is the fastest."

Efficiency was not a specific enough objective to tell the driver which way to go. In this context, "efficient" could mean cheaper or faster, but not both.

Similarly, when understanding the objectives for improving a business process, go a level deeper than efficiency. Consider the following types of objectives:

- turnaround time
- cost
- total effort
- error rate
- revenue generated
- number of sales/customers
- customer satisfaction
- reach/market awareness

While objectives related to the organization's bottom line are common, look for opportunities to include objectives based on the organization's mission or cultural values:

- reduce carbon footprint
- reduce waste
- reduce energy consumption
- increase representation of underrepresented groups
- allocate X% of revenue/profit to community programs
- meet accessibility standards
- support employees' professional development

Considering improvements can involve trade-offs between objectives, so understanding what's most valuable will help the team choose the best possible solutions.

Clear objectives are also measurable, meaning that it's possible to confidently evaluate whether the objective has been met. Quantifiable numbers make a business objective measurable. Both of the sample objectives listed in the previous section have numbers—one objective is to increase sales by 10% and the other is to reduce time spent securing new customers by 10 hours.

In most organizations, measurable objectives pose a challenge. Many organizations do not have solid baseline data to draw from across all areas of the business, nor do they focus on metrics-based performance tracking. In organizations like this, stakeholders asked for measurable objectives simply do not know where to start.

If there are no quantifiable measures, consider using nonspecific yet theoretically measurable business objectives. For example, instead of capturing an objective to "reduce time spent securing new customers by 10 hours," capture an objective like "reduce time spent securing new customers." This doesn't provide a specific target, but it is still theoretically measurable and provides valuable context to the team.

It's also possible to establish measuring and reporting for a specific initiative. For example, a consulting client started a project to convert customers to a new type of contract. The scope included introducing the new offer, identifying target customers, doing email marketing, and having individual sales conversations. Their business objective was a specific conversion rate to the new offering. To measure success, they created a tracking spreadsheet and included a follow-up reporting phase within the project scope. This created metric-focused reporting for the project without adding ongoing tracking to the business.

Focus on Outcomes, Not Scope

Business objectives often start to bleed into the initiative scope by focusing on the solution, not the outcome. Here are some examples that are too solution-oriented to be business objectives:

> *Implement a new customer relationship management (CRM) system.*
>
> *Retool the lead management process to be more efficient.*
>
> *Automate the contract management process using newly available technology.*

Implement, retool, and automate are all solutions—ways of meeting the business objectives. They do not articulate the business objectives themselves. In all these cases, clarity comes from asking the business analyst's favorite question: Why? Or, alternatively, to what end?

- What will be possible once we implement a new CRM?
- How do we measure the efficiency of the lead management process?
- Why is it important to automate the contract management process?

When presented with solutions as business objectives, keep digging into the real problem to be solved. There are ways to do this without being confrontational or sounding like a two-year-old who asks "why, why, why" all the time. We can ask why with finesse—so much so that our stakeholders might not even realize how deep the conversation got and what solution opportunities it surfaced.

> ### *Enhance Your Productivity with Generative AI*
>
> - Request a set of business objectives for the type of solution your stakeholders are proposing.
> - Input your draft business objectives and request refinements or questions to gain clarity.
> - Upload available documents and ask for relevant business objectives.

Gain Alignment on the Business Objectives

With a clear understanding of what effective business objectives look like, let's turn our attention to how to discover expectations from business stakeholders and gain alignment on objectives. There are many techniques for discovering the primary business objectives. Which one you choose will depend heavily on the current state of the business objectives and knowledge of your stakeholder group. If stakeholders quickly reach consensus about the primary objectives and the sponsor is clear about establishing the objectives, the business analyst's role is primarily clarifying and documenting to ensure clear intentions and shared expectations.

In most environments, stakeholders do not show up with a list of well-formed business objectives ready to plop into a document. In fact, they might actively resist the process of clarifying why they want what they want. Stakeholders often have a clear view of their desired solution, whether that's adding a field to a page or transitioning to an entirely new system, but not of their reasons for wanting that solution. In these cases, business analysts must take on a more active role.

Analyze Documents

Before interviewing stakeholders, analyze available documents. This signals respect for the investment stakeholders have already made in documentation and articulating why they want what they want. It's much better to go into a meeting with the sponsor with a clear understanding of the context:

> *I've reviewed the business case you've presented and I think there is an exciting set of opportunities for us to explore. You mentioned a few big-picture objectives. {Summarize them.} As I understand it, in this first project, we're hoping to build a pilot prototype to get customer feedback. Which of these objectives is most important to test at this time?*

Compare the alternative: "Can you tell me why we're doing this work?"

Demonstrating this understanding can also help when the documentation is solution-specific and objectives are poorly defined:

> *I've read the project planning document and I understand everyone is excited about implementing this new CRM. The capabilities of the tool you selected are incredible. What's the most important objective to achieve in the next six months?*

{Listen to the answer, then ask more questions.}

> *That sounds fantastic, what would be possible for your team once that's in place?*

And then keep asking questions until you get to the true problem to be solved.

Sometimes a document already has a list of business objectives. If those objectives are clear and actionable, and if all key stakeholders are aligned on them, focus on confirming alignment and understanding, not reinventing the wheel. The conversation could go like this:

> *I read in the project plan that our business objectives are to increase the number of new customers each month by 10% and reduce the number of hours required by a salesperson to close a new customer by 10 hours. This is clear, and I can facilitate a session to brainstorm possible solution ideas. Before I do, I just want to double-check that everyone agrees about these objectives and we're good to move forward focusing on these for this project.*

Conduct Interviews with Key Stakeholders

When the documentation leaves gaps, interviewing is a great technique to fill them. Individual and small group interviews are both useful for uncovering business objectives.

Individually, you can start by asking questions like these whenever you meet with a new stakeholder:

- What do you expect out of this change effort?
- What do you see as the key business problem to solve or the key business opportunity to meet?
- What is the ultimate financial measure of success?
- What other measures will we use to gauge the success?
- How have you tried to solve this problem before and what was the result of that effort?
- If one thing could change as the result of this project, what would it be?

- How does this project relate to other proposed or active initiatives?
- How does this change effort support the organization's goals?

These questions search for the "why" behind the scope. Why invest financial and staffing resources in this project instead of any number of other potential ideas? Why invest in this initiative instead of doing nothing at all?

In a group interview setting, look for ways to collaborate while also allowing space for different communication styles. A virtual whiteboard where participants add their ideas to sticky notes or upvote each other's suggestions can be a great option. Combining and sorting these ideas can help everyone feel like their input was considered.

While the sponsor and key stakeholders drive business objectives, including users and subject matter experts in interviews provides valuable context to ensure a complete understanding of the problem or opportunity and begins building organization-wide buy-in in the forthcoming changes.

Observe Users and Subject Matter Experts

Some stakeholders, users, and subject matter experts simply don't know why they want what they want—or even what they want! Observation—watching a business user walk through their process—is an effective technique for getting an insider perspective into the problems that need to be solved. It also brings in the perspectives of end users, who may not be advocating for the change but certainly have useful information about the day-to-day challenges with the current product or solution.

Business analysts can observe users in their actual work environment, in a conference room, or remotely using screen-sharing technology.

Ask an end user stakeholder to walk through a typical task. If it's a daily process, they can use examples of work they would be doing that day anyway. As they walk through the process, ask them to describe what they are doing, step-by-step. When it's not clear, ask why they are taking a particular step, such as searching for a piece of information or confirming a detail. Don't try to capture all the details about the process. Focus on getting a good enough understanding to see the problems and opportunities.

Suggest Business Objectives

Once you have reviewed and analyzed all the available information from documents, interviews, and user observation, it's time to suggest business objectives for the change effort. One of my favorite conversation starters is to suggest a few sample business objectives. This is also a reasonable place to start if you have no documentation and get a blank stare when you ask about business objectives.

> *I understand that we're starting a new initiative to implement a CRM system. I've done a bit of research, and typically organizations implementing a CRM are looking to make their sales team more efficient and to improve reporting for each step of the sales process, to give management more visibility into the sales pipeline and revenue projections. Is this what's important to you?*

If the answer is yes, keep going: "Can you tell me more about that?"

If it's no, clarify: "OK, that's great feedback. Is something else motivating you to implement a new CRM at this time?" You might even suggest another option: "Another possibility is that we just want to be on par with other organizations, or that our sales team has expressed frustrations with their existing tools. Is that the case here?"

You'll want to have several possible objectives ready to discuss. Try not to feel attached to any of them. They are merely possibilities and items of curiosity, intended to start a discussion and get to the stakeholder's true desire. Identifying potential business objectives is a great use for generative AI tools.

Alternatively, a conversation with several stakeholders could go like this:

> I know we've been having a bit of trouble gaining
> clarity on business objectives, and we're anxious to
> get started defining the scope. After conversations
> with many of you, I've taken the liberty of drafting
> what I've heard are the primary objectives. Let's read
> through them, and please let me know what you think.

Then you'd review the business objectives section of the document you are working from, encouraging discussion and using the interview questions above to dive deeper into what you hear.

Reconcile Conflicting Expectations

Another aspect of business analysis work is ensuring that all key stakeholders agree on the business objectives, which requires reconciling conflicting expectations about the problem to be solved.

To do this, you must be persistent and facilitate communication and sharing among stakeholders. For example, in a small group interview you might ask each stakeholder to share their opinion on the objectives and back up their opinion with supporting detail or data. As these conversations happen, pay careful attention to any common threads coming up from multiple participants so you can surface these areas of shared interest as a starting point from which to build consensus. Alternatively, you might see that one objective directly or indirectly supports another objective and be able to weave the objectives together into a cohesive intent.

Despite your best efforts, there are some stakeholder environments where no amount of analysis and facilitation will resolve competing interests. At the end of the day, the analyst is leading from the ground up. **The business sponsor owns the final decision about the business objectives and influencing the key stakeholders.** This person may decide to influence others through negotiation, using top-down command, or by incorporating everyone's ideas into the final decision. If it's clear that one or more key stakeholders are not aligned with the sponsor, it's your responsibility to elevate the issue to the sponsor, either directly or through your manager or project manager, and to do as much as possible, given your comfort level and the characteristics of the business environment, to reconcile competing expectations. But at the end of the day, it's the sponsor's responsibility to align all key business stakeholders.

◆≫ Technique in Focus: Process Maps and Business Process Analysis

Mapping business processes is a favorite technique among business analysts. When business objectives are unclear, analyzing the current state (or "as is") business process is a great place to start.

A business process is a repeatable series of steps or activities performed to achieve a desired outcome. Processes deliver consistent value for the organization. They document "how we do it here."

Processes may be performed daily, monthly, quarterly, yearly, or as needed. For example, I've analyzed and documented business processes for reviewing participant workbooks, issuing certificates of completion, and setting up new course sessions. These are activities we do frequently and there is benefit in having a repeatable, documented process. Similarly, the steps a department implements to create a quarterly report or file an annual tax return could be captured as a business process.

There may be multiple paths through a process. Sometimes exceptions and variations come up and business users have to handle those situations. But by and large, there is a repetitive flow from situation A to result B.

Figure 5 shows an example of a business process map including several key features:

- **Process name** – Usually written as verb noun, the name clarifies the action and goal of the process. A common mistake is to use a general name like "Procurement" instead of something specific like, in this case, "Choose Supplier for Procurement Request."
- **Start and end points (ovals)** – Showing clear start and end points limits the scope of the process and narrows your focus.
- **Swim lanes for each role** – These are the horizonal or vertical dividers that show which role performs each activity. Alternatively, list the role in each activity box.
- **Activity Boxes (rectangles)** – Each activity box represents a single step, activity, or discrete item of work performed as part of the process. For clarity, use the verb noun syntax maps, as shown for "Purchase Items" in this example.
- **Lines to show the flow of work** – Lines and arrows capture the process sequence. Each box has a line flowing into it and away from it, tracing the order of the process steps.

Figure 5. A business process map

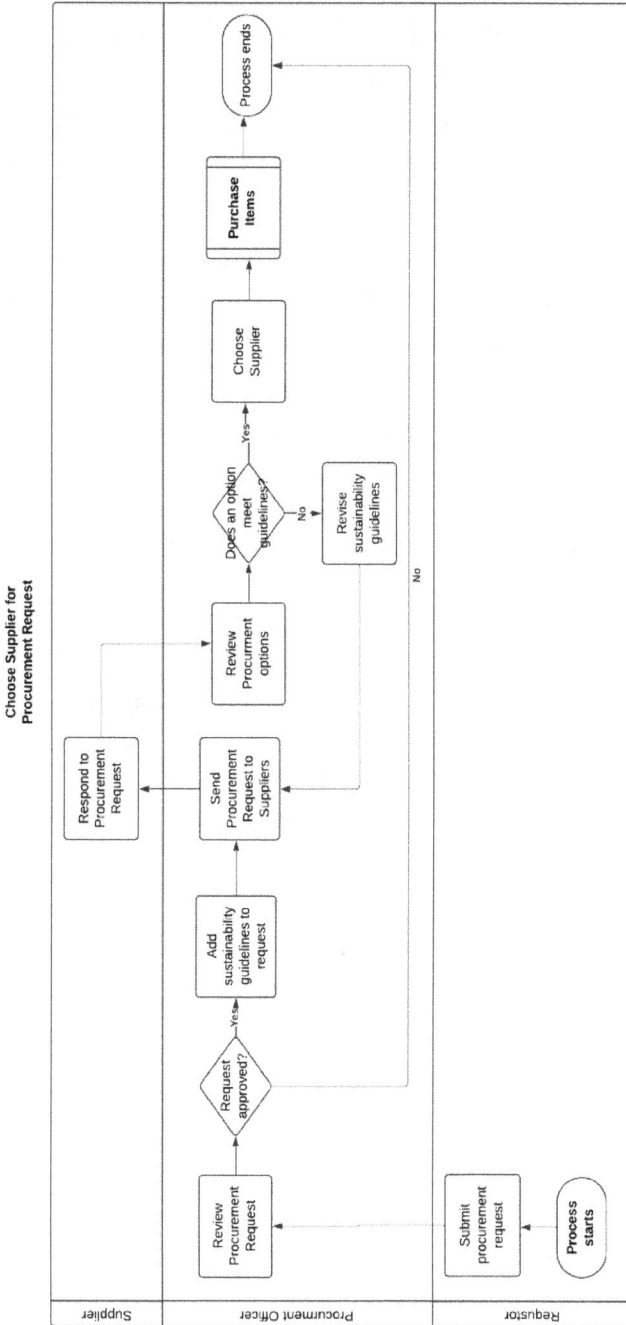

A business process map for choosing a supplier that meets sustainability standards, involving three roles: requestor, procurement officer, and suppler.

- **Decision points (diamonds)** – Decision points show
  variations or alternate paths, and are often phrased as
  questions. Each decision diamond needs at least two lines
  leading away from it (often for yes and no options), and
  those lines should connect either to an activity box or
  another decision diamond.

Using these elements, you can model many types of processes
quickly and easily. Including these elements in process sketches helps
you form a clear high-level understanding of the process and prompt
early feedback from business stakeholders on how the process flows
or should flow.

> In my programs, I also teach a text-based business process
> document that accompanies a process map. While most
> business analysts only use process maps, when they work
> with a text-based template they find that the additional
> detail and critical thinking it requires prompts deeper
> analysis that is less likely to overlook nuances and exceptions.
> The downloadable Business Analyst Success Pack includes
> an annotated business process document template.
> Download it here: www.bridging-the-gap.com/successpack.

Business process mapping is a foundational skill used throughout
a change effort. It helps analysts achieve multiple possible outcomes.

Mapping the high-level business process will help stakeholders
align on business objectives and will build clarity on potential problems to solve. Consider a scenario where the sponsor has suggested
the following objectives:

*Reduce customer service inquiries about missing
shipments by 50%.*

Fix the shipment process.

I encourage you to evaluate what could be improved about these objectives before reading further.

The first objective is clear, but it needs more context to be actionable. The second objective is actually a solution. A proactive business analyst could ask more questions about these objectives, but might find the discussions go in circles without any clear answers. Another approach is to discover the current state of the shipment process, and potentially take an even higher-level view by looking at the processes around order deliveries that could lead to customer service inquiries about missed shipments. Creating process maps for the "Ship Order" and "Respond to Inquiries" processes, plus any key processes that happen in between and perhaps even processes that happen before shipping, will reveal the big-picture context of the current state.

There is a latent assumption in these objectives that the inquiries are caused by problems in the shipment process. But what if the root cause is in the shipment notifications or the way the shipping address is collected during the order? What if the way inquiries are tracked makes it seem like there is a problem when there isn't? That would be a relatively rare outcome, but stranger things have happened! You will not see all the interrelated aspects of business functions or be able to determine the true root cause of a problem unless you look at the entire scope of the process.

Analyzing the current-state business process also breaks down communication barriers between departments and resolves misunderstandings that create different views of what the problem is. Process mapping creates a shared understanding of the problem because people see how the work they do impacts people from downstream departments.

It's also not uncommon for business process problems to almost solve themselves through a current-state analysis. The problem becomes clear and obvious to everyone involved, and the solution is so simple that people can't help but implement it right away. When this happens, it's a brilliant day to showcase the value of business analysis. Everyone likely expected the solution to cost a lot more and take way more time. When you find a simple and obvious process adjustment, claim it as a huge win! Celebrate your team, and celebrate your contribution to uncovering this improvement.

No matter how you use business process mapping, it creates tremendous value for your organization. It can elevate you into a business analyst role or catapult you forward in your career. Examples abound. Let me just share two.

Jeannie was part of The Business Analyst Blueprint® training program. After mapping her first business process and receiving confidence-building feedback, she was asked to create workflows for all her company's accounting and underwriting processes as part of a system migration effort. This avoided a $40,000 investment in an outside vendor and catapulted Jeannie into an opportunity to expand her knowledge of the business and increase her credibility with stakeholders. Going forward, the IT director requested to work directly with her.

A $40,000 savings is significant for most IT budgets. Just imagine the leverage Jeannie had going into her next salary negotiation, not to mention the increase in job security. This is, of course, on top of the opportunity to do strategic, high-impact business analysis work on a highly visible initiative.

Then there is Perry, who was in between positions. Perry wasn't new to process mapping, but still found opportunities to improve his skill set. He also volunteered with a nonprofit organization to build additional on-the-job experience, which he was able to speak to during his interview. Soon after completing the program, he landed not one but two job offers.

I could share many, many more examples, and will in later chapters. What matters now is that this one technique can add a lot of value and transform your career. If you haven't mapped a business process lately, perhaps now is the time to revisit this necessary skill set.

Enhance Your Productivity with Generative AI

- Share the known business process steps (or even just the process name) and ask for missing steps and alternative flows.
- Use an AI-enabled visual modeling tool to create a draft process map.
- Upload several process maps and ask for redundancies, inconsistencies, and other opportunities for improvement.
- Upload detailed procedural or training documents and request a high-level process map.

✅ Success Strategy: Invest in Stakeholder Relationships

In Step 1, you identified key stakeholders. Step 2 is an ideal time to make stakeholder relationships a conscious priority, setting up habits and fostering relationships that will grow and open up possibilities as the work unfolds. Stakeholder relationships are your most valuable currency as a business analyst. A stakeholder who knows you, likes you, and trusts you is more likely to show up to your meetings on time, defend you when you aren't in the room, and answer your questions to the best of their ability. No matter how good you are, there will come a day when your team misses a requirement and you need to take quick and decisive action to address it. Strong stakeholder relationships are the currency you need to schedule a meeting at the last minute and get people to drop other important work and focus on the change.

Later in the initiative you might have to push back on stakeholders based on the scope and the constraints of the budget or timeline.

At this stage, you are in an ideal position to understand all their pain points and the positive possibilities they see, which makes this an ideal time to demonstrate that you deserve their trust and respect.

Investing in stakeholder relationships is an ongoing activity. Every interaction, every document, every email is an opportunity to cultivate stakeholder relationships. Here's a list of ideas to consider and act on:

- Take time while discovering the business objectives to listen to your stakeholders and facilitate communication between stakeholder groups.
- Demonstrate through listening and analysis that you care about their needs, perceptions, problems, and ideas.
- Go out of your way to set aside your own biases and expectations so you can absorb what they have to share.
- Be clear about your intentions and follow through on your commitments.
- Hear out their concerns about their fellow stakeholders, but don't join the rumor mill.
- Be discreet about what you share and how you share it.

Invest in stakeholder relationships now and you'll see much more positive momentum in your discussions, decisions, and meetings.

In virtual, hybrid, and global settings, being intentional about building relationships is even more important and often requires concerted effort. Leverage the moments before and after meetings, schedule personal discussions, use internal messaging systems, and take advantage of any travel and virtual social opportunities.

As you work to build trust with your stakeholders and understand how they see problems and opportunities, it's easy to make a very common mistake—creating the perception that you will solve every problem they discuss with you. Active listening and deep understanding build engagement, but stakeholders may confuse understanding with commitment and you are not in the position to commit to solving any specific problems yet.

To avoid this problem, clarify your role and next steps early and often. For example, you might say something like this when starting a meeting:

> *Today we're going to talk about the business objectives*
> *we hope this initiative will fulfill. I want to hear as much*
> *as possible about the problems you face related to*
> *X and the opportunities you see to achieve Y. I can't*
> *promise that we'll be able to act on everything we talk*
> *about today, but if we have as open a conversation as*
> *possible, I'll be in the best position to help you realize*
> *as many of your goals as we can within the constraints*
> *that have been laid out.*

This clearly sends the message that you are listening but not promising.

Then at the end of the meeting, you might remind participants about the outcome:

> *Wow. This was a great discussion. Thank you for*
> *diving so deep and sharing so much information with*
> *such honesty. I really appreciate you taking the time*
> *to be here today. As I mentioned at the beginning of*
> *our meeting, I can't promise that we'll solve every*
> *problem we discussed, but I know we generated some*
> *great ideas and I hope we'll be able to address many*
> *of them. I can promise that I will capture every idea*
> *you brought to the table and work with the implemen-*
> *tation team to include as many as possible within the*

scope. As we get further into defining the solution, you'll have the opportunity to further prioritize so we are sure to address what you see as the most valuable needs.

As a next step, I'll send out meeting notes so you can be sure I didn't miss anything. I'll also draft the business objectives section of our scope statement. You'll have the opportunity to review this before we finalize it. Our next meeting will involve looking at various solution approaches so we can address as many of your concerns as possible. Does anyone have any questions for me about next steps?

This closing accomplishes many objectives. First, it clarifies your next step, which is part of being clear about your role and building trust. Second, it helps create commitment from your stakeholders, because you clearly articulate that they will continue to have input and decision-making power. Third, and perhaps most importantly, it clarifies that you aren't promising anything but that you will do what you can to accomplish as much as possible.

Managing expectations and building momentum is crucial to cultivating long-term stakeholder relationships and building your professional credibility.

▶ Next Steps

Business analysis is all about creating positive change. Uncovering the expected outcomes is essential to expanding your value as a business analyst. If you are working toward undesired outcomes, your contribution will not have the positive impact you want.

No matter what methodology your organization uses or what deliverables you are expected to create, clearly defined business objectives give you a target to work toward. And the more your sponsors and stakeholders are aligned on these objectives, the less noise and unproductive conflict you'll have to deal with throughout the initiative.

Here are some next steps to implement what you've learned:

- Identify two to five clear, actionable business objectives that focus on the why, not the what, of the change effort.
- Navigate any resistance you might face by analyzing documents, interviewing stakeholders and subject matter experts, observing business users, and making suggestions.
- Reconcile conflicting expectations so the team has clarity and alignment around the business objectives.
- Analyze the current state of the business process to further clarify the opportunities and problems to solve.
- Invest in stakeholder relationships to create positive momentum in your future discussions, decisions, and meetings.

Understanding what success looks like will help you avoid so many possible missteps and focus your efforts on actual business value. Even if your organization doesn't ask you to discover or document the business objectives, use these approaches to ask better questions and establish context before diving into details. And if you get lost in the details, come back to these questions. They will help you find your way.

Discovering the primary business objectives sets the stage for defining scope, ensuring that you don't end up with a solution that solves the wrong problem or, even worse, a solution that no one can measure to determine whether it's successful.

3

Define Scope

After I speak at an event, at least a few people usually come up to ask the "real" questions—the kind that feel scary to share in front of the group. Often these questions are about the obstacles and frustrations that keep us from doing what we know we should be doing. If we are lucky enough to meet in person, please say hello and ask me that deep dark question that's been bugging you. I can almost guarantee I've heard it before.

Once, after a presentation on stakeholder engagement, an attendee asked a question that caught me off guard. He had been told he was too business-oriented. How could that be possible if his title was *business* analyst?

As I typically do, I asked a lot of follow-up questions to get to the root cause. Why did he think the team might see him as too business-oriented? What were his business analysis practices? What challenges was the team facing?

It turned out that this business analyst was great at understanding the frustrations and needs of the business stakeholders and building strong relationships with them. But then, instead of balancing their needs and desires within the constraints, he took on their issues and became their advocate. He didn't prioritize requests or keep a parking lot of lower-priority items to get to later. This created *a lot* of friction between him and the technology stakeholders.

Although it's important to uncover the needs of the business, balance those needs within the constraints of the initiative. That's how business analysts define a clear scope for the solution a specific change effort will implement. This often means taking on what might feel like a fraction of what the business wants to deliver an initial value-creating solution.

That's the core of Step 3 of the Business Analysis Process—defining the scope. A clear and complete statement of scope gives your project team the direction they need to realize the business needs. Scope makes the business needs tangible so multiple team participants can see ways to contribute. Scope becomes a touchstone guiding the subsequent steps of the Business Analysis Process and the effort of other participants.

Clarifying what's in and out of scope and what success looks like before jumping into the details is one way a business analyst can provide strategic leadership. To achieve this, analysts must facilitate conversations with key decision-makers and build robust partnerships between stakeholder groups across the business and technology teams.

This process step focuses on the scope of the solution implemented by the current change effort. The goal is to maximize the value delivered within the allotted budget and on schedule while considering any other constraints.

A clear scope narrows the team's focus so they can gain positive momentum and deliver value to the business.

Explore Solution Options

Solutions fulfill business objectives, solve business problems, or address new opportunities. Working with business stakeholders to understand their problems and opportunities will often generate more solution ideas than the project can support. Develop the big picture first and then work with your implementation team to decide which part of the solution to implement first, achieve a positive ROI, and support the case for future investments (or free up resources for other value-creating initiatives).

Before we dive into how to choose a solution approach, let's consider the types of solution options that a team can generally consider.

Process Improvements

Business process improvements are often the most cost-effective to implement and the most likely to be overlooked. Assuming that every improvement requires some sort of software-based solution leads teams to overlook many options. There is no need to automate a process step that you can eliminate. And often, streamlining a process achieves is simpler and more effective than investing in new software or features.

For example, Wendy was in a software development role when she mapped a labor-intensive and error-prone deployment process within her department that the developers really wanted to automate. Led by her analysis, the team uncovered multiple ways to streamline the manual process, minimize the errors, and significantly decrease the effort required. When they were done, automation no longer made sense. Wendy saved her company countless days (or perhaps even weeks or months) automating a process that just needed tweaks. She also got to present her work to a leadership team, which raised her profile within the company. As a result of this work, the organization promoted Wendy into a business analyst role.

Value-driven business analysts can also use process improvements to generate quick wins early in a big initiative, to test assumptions, and to build buy-in and engagement with business stakeholders across the organization.

Business process improvements can take many forms:

- **Clarifying the business process.** Analyzing the current state will naturally resolve differences, creating a shared understanding of process flows and ways to improve handoffs. This awareness can lead to self-corrections in the current process. Celebrate these quick wins, even though they might seem too obvious; they can build project momentum and improve engagement.

- **Eliminating unnecessary steps.** In general, eliminate before you automate. Why invest in automating unnecessary work? Consider whether each step in the process contributes to the desired outcome or adds value. Look for duplicate tasks, unnecessary communication, and excessive effort to avoid exceptions that could be handled differently.

- **Shifting work.** Look for ways to optimize timeline, cost, or both by shifting work to different roles. For example, refactoring a process may leave one person involved for the sake of one trivial activity. Shifting that detail to the role that does the set of activities before or after could free that person up and save time. In other situations, splitting activities across two roles may leverage different skill sets more cost-effectively. In my business, I have people help me with logistical course questions and technical setup so I can focus on preparing course materials, providing on-the-job coaching, and creating new content.

- **Developing work aids.** Look for opportunities to create reusable templates, scripts, or checklists that can make the process faster and more consistent. When possible, build these work aids into the technology platform; for example, by building canned responses for frequently asked questions into the ticket management system.

Starting your analysis with a high-level process map will help the team uncover opportunities like these.

Software Solutions

When considering software as part of the solution to business problems or opportunities, start by asking what the software needs to do. Keeping in mind the business objectives and your understanding of the business process, brainstorm a list of features or high-level capabilities that would benefit the organization. For example, consider this list of possible capabilities, or features,[5] for a course delivery system:

- Create a course
- Create lessons within a course
- Organize lessons into modules
- Upload videos to lessons
- Track course participant's progress through the course
- Enable participants to ask questions about a lesson
- Notify instructors when a participant asks a question

Software can enable many different capabilities:

- **Automating a business process.** Software can replicate a series of manual steps, reducing or eliminating a business user's work.
- **Managing a process workflow.** Software can guide a business user's manual work, perhaps by replacing paper forms, triggering process steps, and automatically following up on handoffs. In this case the business user may still

---

[5] One terminology note here: I and many other business analysts and project professionals use the term "feature" for a high-level list of categories of functional requirements. These are not the specific, implementable functional requirements. However, others use the term "feature" to describe a granular requirement.

complete certain manual steps, but more accurately and with less human oversight.

- **Sharing data between systems.** If the manual aspect of the process involves inputting data from one system into another system, or retrieving information from multiple systems, integrating the systems or passing data between them can provide a lot of business value.
- **Generating reports.** Automated reports allow users to share information with other departments, projects, or organizations without running manual queries or compiling data from multiple sources.
- **Enabling self-service.** Businesses can reduce overhead by giving customers direct access to key information and even enabling them to complete aspects of a business process independently. Online shopping is one example.

Digitizing a process often requires new capabilities such as setting up users, managing permissions, handling service disruptions and exceptions, and supporting customers. When analyzing the features stakeholders want, business analysts should articulate these dependencies and impacts.

When analyzing customer-facing software projects, think of these products in the context of customer processes rather than business processes. For example, social media provides an alternative way to share pictures with friends and family, and communication tools like Voxer and WhatsApp enable groups of people to communicate without email.

Great products solve unmet needs. Often these are needs a customer never even thought of, but once the feature is available it improves their life so much that they can't imagine doing without it. Imagine how amazing email seemed when fax machines were the primary way of sending documents electronically. (Not to mention how great fax machines seemed in comparison to snail mail.) And not to take us too off track, but there was a time when even writing a letter was a new technology and the printing press replaced manually copying books by hand.

Some business-focused professionals shy away from getting too involved in software changes and thus say no to career-enhancing opportunities, often based on the perception that they need to be able to write software code and do other technical tasks that are outside their core skill set. Software applications are simply tools that run according to our instructions. We just need to be very specific about what we want them to do. The business analyst's role is just to help the team get clear on what the software needs to do. It's up to the software developer or systems designer to figure out how to build the solution.

There are several ways to leverage software to enable new capabilities for the business. Here are the most common options:

- **Develop custom software.** This is a rare option as of this writing, and often reserved for proprietary software that gives a company a competitive advantage or is part of a product sold to customers. Even in those cases, it's common to leverage third-party applications as part of the custom development.
- **Use third-party applications,** also called COTS (commercial-off-the-shelf systems) or SaaS (software as a service). These solutions are currently the norm. As the number and quality of third-party applications increases and it becomes easier to customize them, it's becoming increasingly common to incorporate third-party applications in a solution approach. While these applications require a financial investment to purchase or license, they are often easier to implement and customize than a custom software solution.

- **Leverage existing software capabilities.** Sometimes the organization has already deployed a solution that includes the needed capabilities in a different context. Many third-party systems have multiple configuration options. Before looking for a new system, it's always a good idea to evaluate existing software and systems.
- **Update an existing system.** Similarly, sometimes it's simpler to add a new feature to an existing software system than to implement a new system.
- **Customize a third-party application.** In some situations, it makes sense to work directly with the vendor to build a new feature into software the organization already uses.
- **Integrate two or more systems**. If the company has existing systems that each incorporate part of the desired feature set, integrating these systems can be a cost-effective alternative to developing new software.

Any business problem and set of features will have multiple solution options. When time allows, explore as many options as possible with the solution team before proposing a solution approach. The most common scenario, though, is working within an existing solution framework. If the organization has already invested in a set of tools, the change effort often assumes that the solution will work within that framework. For example, many business analysts specialize in applications such as Salesforce, ServiceNow, and SAP. It would be inefficient and unproductive to explore all possible business applications every time a business user asks to add a new field or tweak a workflow.

However, it still makes sense to explore multiple solution options within the existing application, as there are often multiple ways to achieve the objective. There may also be trade-offs between optimizing the business process and expanding software capabilities to automate or manage that process, or opportunities to build integration points between systems.

Once the existing tool set is outdated or can no longer meet business objectives, or a new set of business objectives requires an entirely new set of capabilities that existing tools do not support, then it is certainly time to start building a business case for a larger initiative to replace the existing system.

Generative AI

Generative AI solutions present new options for meeting business objectives. Unlike traditional software solutions that rely on coded instructions and detailed business rules, generative AI software solutions can complete more flexible tasks, such as drafting written communication, summarizing content, designing new solutions, and simulating possibilities.

AI has the potential to unlock tremendous possibilities, but there are many considerations too—ethics, the suitability of the data set, privacy issues, and copyright issues, to list just a few. Business analysts can help businesses focus on using generative AI to create value in meaningful ways by asking questions:

- What possibilities do AI solutions create for our organization?
- What AI capabilities are our business applications building into their software? How would those create value for our organization?
- What data can we leverage to train an AI system? What are the strengths and limitations of that data?
- Where do we trust the output of an AI system and where to we want to incorporate human reviews and interventions?

- How can we combine our human intelligence and generative AI to unlock new opportunities?
- Where can we leverage generative AI for automation and efficiency?
- How will we leverage the human thinking power and creativity that's freed up by implementing generative AI solutions?

Research, experimentation, and ongoing learning and development are essential. Changes are unfolding quickly, creating new tools, capabilities, and opportunities.

Choose the Solution Approach

While there are always many possible solution options, deciding on the best solution approach for a specific initiative is a collaborative effort that the business analyst either leads or participants in. Often, stakeholders already have a solution idea. This can be a good starting point for more questions:

- Now that we understand the business objectives, does the proposed solution option still make sense?
- Will the solution achieve our objectives?
- Should we explore any other options before making a final decision?

When deciding on a solution approach, collaborating with business and technology stakeholders ensures the approach is feasible and is leveraging the organization's available technology. Ideally, the decision team will include a lead developer or technical architect, a project manager, and someone to represent the business (such as the product manager, product owner, business lead, and/or primary subject matter experts). Including multiple perspectives will generate the best possible ideas.

On my first project, which involved selling and delivering ebooks in an integrated online platform, I received the so-called gift of time—about three months to work with the product manager to understand the business objectives and requirements before the project officially started and the implementation team got involved. While this might sound appealing, it's difficult to use this time effectively, something we'll talk about in the next chapter. As a first-time business analyst, I didn't realize how collaboration engaged the team in buying into the change. Since I was coming from a black box testing role in quality assurance, I did understand the high-level system architecture. So I made the mistake of figuring out the overall system architecture of the solution by myself.

When the project manager got the team together for the kick-off, I stood up in front of all 20 experienced developers and presented my brilliant technical solution. You can probably imagine the responses! "That won't work." "Why are you designing the system? That's our job." I knew my approach would achieve the business intent, but I got the message and took a big step back. Instead, we focused on why the feature was a priority, to gain buy-in. Then we created use cases and wireframes to describe the necessary functionality, and finally we agreed on the design for the web application and database to accomplish it.

In the end, the team came up with the same technical solution I proposed. The difference was, now they bought into building it because it was their solution. And I learned a career-changing lesson in collaboration: In business analysis, being right is less important than taking your team on the journey. Having the best ideas can be less significant than creating room for the entire team to be part of the idea creation process.

This is the time to get subject matter experts and technical experts involved in the project and to start bringing in more perspectives and ideas. As I learned, the best way to get stakeholders bought into the process improvement effort is to involve them in the discovery and analysis required to improve it.

Instead of making an assumption, ask a question.

Instead of choosing the best idea that comes to you, ask for input.

Instead of relying on your knowledge, ask for clarification.

Making stakeholder involvement your default way of identifying solution options will make it easier to get buy-in on the changes. Here are some of the elicitation and discovery techniques you can use to explore possible solution options with stakeholders:

- **Brainstorming.** Open the session by sharing the business objectives, establish ground rules, and invite participants to offer ideas. Remember that introverted participants benefit when given time to reflect independently. Build in pauses and rotate participation to ensure everyone can contribute. In a virtual setting, experiment with having participants add ideas to a virtual whiteboard. Plan for time after brainstorming to evaluate the ideas.

- **Prototyping and high-level process maps.** When your stakeholders struggle to envision new solutions, create a sample wireframe and high-level business process map of how the solution *could* work. For example, an analyst prototyping an applicant tracking system for recruiters might show them how they could see a list of job applications that were automatically sorted and scored. Or, imagine a high-level process map with new steps added for a coordinator to schedule interviews and follow up with candidates, to help an overworked hiring manager see how they can receive more support. The idea is not to get the solution right but to prompt discussion about what's possible.

- **Research.** Identify alternative solution options by exploring existing systems, requesting trials, getting demos, analyzing help and system documentation, and benchmarking against competitors. Generative AI can be a great research companion too. Collaboration is still key, so build in cycles to share findings and get feedback.

- **Leveraging Constraints.** While it might seem that constraints would reduce the number of ideas, often the reverse is true. Human creativity excels under constrained scenarios. My daughter loves to do "three-color contests." She picks three random markers or colored pencils and creates a picture with just those colors. It's amazing what she creates, and it's usually not a picture she would have drawn if she had access to the whole box of markers. Be clear about project constraints such as the tech stack, business application, best practices, organizational standards, timelines, resources, or budget. Then ask how you can deliver the most possible value within those constraints. That's a powerful way to help your team find answers!

No matter what techniques you choose, collaboration is essential. When people feel like they are part of developing the solution they are much more likely to buy into it and participate in implementing it.

Conduct Impact Analysis

As part of exploring a solution approach, be sure to understand how that solution impacts other areas of the business, other business systems, and system integrations. The initial business sponsor usually doesn't consider these impacts, and this is part of the value that a business analyst can provide.

On this same ebook project, I uncovered a major impact that no business analyst on my team had ever dealt with before—one that wasn't clearly articulated in the original scope. Historically, our business model was selling access to an online content product as a single unit. For this product, the product manager wanted our customers to be able to choose which reference ebooks were included in their online access. This required an entirely different fulfillment and customer service process.

As part of exploring solution options, I worked with a VP-level stakeholder on the print book fulfillment side who managed an entirely different set of business applications. We found a way to use that system to track the sale of ebooks and to send the ebook sales data to the online content delivery system so libraries could access their ebook catalog through the online database. Of course, this is basic functionality now, but at the time our organization had never delivered this type of solution. By uncovering this impact early, we had plenty of time to design a long-term solution.

Always ask what impact the solution could have—on other business applications, other departments, and other business processes. Techniques like system context diagrams, end-to-end business process mapping, and architectural reviews can help bring system impacts to the forefront.

Another way to think about this is to consider the assumptions in the project. What must be true or in place for each feature to be viable? Are there any dependencies or impacts that haven't been considered? An impact analysis checklist that lists each system and key business process area can be a great help here.

One set of impacts that is often overlooked is changes to the business process itself. It's safe to assume that just about any technology change impacts the business process in some way. For example, perhaps in the current state a customer service representative sends an email to notify a salesperson that an account has been canceled. As part of defining the solution approach, the team determines that software can handle this notice automatically on the sales dashboard. In this case, the Cancel Account business process needs to be updated to reflect the change, and both the customer service and sales team members need to be trained accordingly.

Often, automation efforts will create new manual steps to complete, such as processing exceptions. For example, there are many online scheduling tools today that could be used to have a job applicant schedule their own interview based on the hiring manager's availability, saving a lot of back-and-forth. But what if the applicant never schedules their interview? Should there be another outreach? If so, who is responsible for the communication, how long do they wait, and how do they know who to reach out to?

The value of this work is in uncovering these upstream and downstream impacts early, so they don't become significant issues that derail the project late in implementation—the "missed requirements" that so many teams complain about. But impact analysis often invalidates the original sponsor's assumption that the solution will be simple. They may need to negotiate with other senior-level stakeholders for the priority and to get more people on board with their vision. It also expands the project budget, and the sponsor may have to reduce their feature list to accommodate the impacts within the time and cost constraints.

It's easy to get caught in the middle of these discussions and start advocating on behalf of the original sponsor when working with stakeholders from impacted departments. A best practice is to have the sponsor pave the path and ensure all participants agree on the initiative's priority. On that ebook project, after we identified the high-level impacts, I worked with a small team: one stakeholder representing fulfillment and a technical expert who was building most of the integration, looping in a high-level stakeholder from the print side as needed. But before we started work, the product manager and project manager made a clear case for the priority and laid out the overall vision to get everyone on board.

Enhance Your Productivity with Generative AI

- Share the business objectives and ask AI for solution options.
- Upload your current-state business processes and ask for optimization ideas.
- Experiment with and test solution ideas.
- Provide context and ask for potential impacts.

Prioritize Requirements

In most organizations, the team does not actually own project scope. They own managing the scope and collaborating with stakeholders to define the scope, but the sponsor and high-level stakeholders own the scope. They decide what's in and out and whether to approve the initiative. The implementation team provides analysis on solution options and trade-offs.

When the team fully understands the business needs, identifies possible solution approaches, and defines the key features or requirements that will address the business objectives, the initiative often grows larger. As a result, many ideas may not fit into the scope. Prioritization is key to ensuring that the most valuable work gets the most attention and maximizing the project's ROI.

Ensuring that each requirement or capability links back to the business objectives provides a first level of prioritization. This can happen through review and discussion or by explicitly linking requirements to objectives using a matrix. If idea generation went wide, this step alone could narrow scope tremendously. But often, initiatives require more prioritization and focus. Engaging the business stake-holders in these decisions, while sometimes difficult, gives them a say in which requirements are most valuable.

There are several ways to prioritize requirements:

- **High/Medium/Low.** Label each requirement 1 (high priority), 2 (medium), or 3 (low priority).
- **Rank Priority.** Since business stakeholders tend to consider every requirement a high priority, a more rigorous approach is to rank the requirements. Most agile environments rank the product backlog by business priority.
- **Sort Then Rank.** Combining these techniques works well: Sort requirements into relatively even buckets of high, medium, and low priority first and then rank the high-priority items. This saves time and energy because ranking low-priority features has diminishing returns.
- **Voting.** When there are multiple stakeholders, a voting strategy can help. Give each person 100 votes to cast (or "dollars" to spend) across 10 potential features and then add the votes each feature gets to determine a consolidated priority list.

Prioritization gets easier when everyone understands the potential timelines and costs of each feature. It's a bit like looking at the price tag before decide whether you want the sweater. When I'm prioritizing ideas for the next three months, I always identify a priority and a level of effort for each idea and categorize them in relation to our strategic vision and goals. High-priority, low-effort items ("quick wins") aligned with our big-picture vision get sorted to the top of the list.[6]

---

[6] Download the Quick Wins Assessment as part of the Business Analyst Success Pack here: www.bridging-the-gap.com/successpack.

Sometimes stakeholders' priorities shift once they understand what it takes to implement each capability. A feature might seem like a priority until it reaches a certain threshold or threatens to delay a change effort. This is one reason not to make promises to the business team early in the project. When exploring business needs and solution approaches, emphasize that you are in discovery mode, not commitment mode. Ultimately, the sponsors or executive stakeholders are responsible for making these decisions. The business analyst's role, in collaboration with the implementation team, is to present the viable options and clarify the impacts of different decisions. The business analyst can also help the sponsor make the case for extending the timeline or increasing the investment by helping them communicate the business needs and value of the project to other executives.

If the project can't get more resources, give the business sponsor options. This helps reframe the often unspoken but deeply felt resentment that the technology team is simply not building what the business wants. While technology stakeholders rarely deliberately withhold features or decide something is out of scope, they often make decisions about what to cut when facing time pressures. Ultimately, the role of technology stakeholders is to provide input on effort, timelines, technical feasibility, and the long-term costs associated with solution options, to inform meaningful business decisions. The role of the business is to make the often difficult choices about where to invest given the constraints.

Expanding scope often has impacts beyond the current initiative and requires a perspective that considers the impact to other organizational priorities—typically a program manager or strategic steering committee. There is a huge career opportunity for business analysts to get involved in these types of decisions. The better a business analyst is at helping the business focus on the most valuable features within the scope of an initiative, the more they demonstrate an ability to balance business value with budget constraints. That skill set gets business analysts noticed and can create opportunities to work on more strategic decisions at the level of project portfolios or value streams.

Craft a Scope Statement

Once the team understands the business objectives, explores solution options, chooses an approach, and prioritizes requirements according to business value, it's time to crystallize everything in a clear, concise scope statement that captures these decisions. The statement should define terms and provide context, and ideally include visual models, ensuring that both business and technology stakeholders can easily understand it.

Although this section considers the scope statement as a stand-alone document, this information often appears in other documents or deliverables. Common examples include a business case or business requirements document, software requirements specification, project plan, project charter, or an agile epic. Often, adding a section to an existing document is easier than adding a new deliverable to an established process.

Whether the scope statement is a stand-alone document or a portion of one or more of the other project documents, double-check that it includes at least these key elements:

- overview
- business objectives
- capabilities
- assumptions
- constraints
- out of scope
- visual models (optional)

This outline follows the template provided in the downloadable Business Analyst Success Pack. The resulting document is only a few pages long, and summarizes the outcome of the collaborative and analysis work the team has completed. It may also include contextual information such as a purpose statement, list of stakeholders, or list of actors.

Overview

An overview is a high-level summary of the scope of the initiative, describing the why, what, and how in two or three sentences. Consider it an elevator pitch: If you met an executive in an elevator and had one minute to describe your current project, what would you say? Being ready with this kind of summary for any current work is a great career strategy. You never know when you'll bump into someone who can support your work or career!

To illustrate, are a few hypothetical overviews for different project types. First, consider this overview from a home insurance provider:

> *We want to support the efficiency of our claim agents and reduce the number of follow-up calls from homeowners and contractors checking on the status of their claims and repairs. This project involves building a mobile application that will support all aspects of the on-site claims process, integrate with our customer service software, and provide online support to homeowners and contractors so they can view the status of all aspects of their claim and upload supporting documentation.*

In just two sentences, this clearly explains the business objectives, chosen solution, and new capabilities being enabled.

Next, consider this overview for a nonprofit organization:

> *Pricing and support for our current customer*
> *relationship management system have become too*
> *costly and time-intensive for our small, nimble team,*
> *particularly given the limited functionality we currently*
> *use. Our goal is to replace our current application with*
> *[New Application]. The new solution will provide donor*
> *management, follow-up, proposal management,*
> *and customer service, and will integrate with our*
> *accounting system for billing and accounts receivable*
> *information. It could also enable us to deploy*
> *peer-to-peer fundraising tools in the future.*

Again, this three-sentence summary outlines why the change effort is happening, what will change, and the essential capabilities needed from the new solution, as well as some additional features that could benefit the organization long-term.

Business Objectives

After the overview comes a section describing the initiative's specific business objectives or benefits. This list of three to five discrete business objectives provides a clear sense of the desired outcome of the initiative.

Make sure the business objectives are consistent with the overview. This might seem obvious, but it's easy to get off track when exploring solution options and the different outcomes they can support. Creating the scope statement provides a good opportunity to check alignment. For example, the home insurance mobile application might have the following business objectives:

Reduce the average time a claim agent spends preparing and submitting a claim from 8 hours to 6 hours or less.

Reduce follow-up calls by homeowners to check on claim status by 50%.

Reduce follow-up calls by contractors by 50%.

Increase homeowner adoption of the web application by 30%.

As you explore solutions, new objectives can emerge:

While not the initial intent of this project, this new solution also raises the possibility of reducing the overall cost of a claim by more easily facilitating competing bids.

Other times, a solution puts a foundational piece in place that enables future business objectives:

By capturing original, high-quality digital images and video walk-throughs and the costs associated with specific types of claims, we'll be building a data repository that we can use to improve claim projections.

Capabilities

The capabilities list identifies specific solution elements to be implemented or considered for implementation, and can include both software and business capabilities. Keep these at a high level for now; the team will refine them in Step 5, "Define the Detailed Requirements." For example, the scope statement for the home insurance mobile application could list the following capabilities:

- *Claims agent can complete all aspects of preparing and submitting a claim, including:*
  - o *video walk-through*
  - o *supporting images*
  - o *complete claim documentation*
- *Customer can upload supporting documentation such as quotes and invoices to the claim*
- *Contractor can upload supporting documentation such as insurance, quotes, and invoices to the claim*
- *Customer and contractor can create and update profile information that can be reused across claims*
- *Review the current claim documentation requirements and business rules and explore opportunities to simplify them*

The first four capabilities are software features while the last is a business process capability.

Assumptions

Assumptions are factors believed to be true, but not confirmed; for example, that an existing system has a particular feature or that customers will react positively to a new feature.

Documenting assumptions brings them to light and invites a negative response. If the business analyst assumes something and a team member believes the assumption is incorrect, that's a risk the business analyst wants to be aware of and proactively manage.

Assumptions can be a significant factor in the business analysis planning effort we'll uncover in Step 4, because you may want to tackle the features related to risky assumptions earlier in the process. As the analysis unfolds, poke and prod at the assumptions, either confirming their validity or invalidating them so new plans can be made. For now, clearly articulate any assumptions so they aren't hidden in meeting notes or side discussions. Be attentive: Assumptions tend to surface during discussions about business objectives and scope.

Constraints

Constraints—restrictions or limitations on possible solutions—can have a dramatic impact on scope. Constraints can be business or technical in nature. The budget, time restrictions, and technical architecture decisions are all examples of constraints.

The ebook project mentioned earlier included one subsystem that was particularly challenging to update because it was used by every one of the 30+ products supported by the technology team. Any project that required an update to this subsystem had to wait for a release. That meant extensive regression testing, schedules that were tied to otherwise unrelated projects, and steep increases in budget and resources. Almost every scope statement in that organization started with a constraint saying that changes to this subsystem would not be required.

Anytime a developer mentioned that a particular feature or solution approach would require an update to this underlying system, an ominous hush would fall over the room. All attention would turn to the product manager with the following aura: Is this feature really that important? If the answer was yes, then the project manager would often reluctantly ask, "When's the next release and is it too late to get aboard the release train?" Overstepping this constraint prompted a major scope change, and was treated accordingly.

Watch for constraints and build them into your collaboration process.

Out of Scope

The "out of scope" section identifies any items that have been discussed but excluded from the initiative. This might be the most vital section, as it sets expectations about what's not included. This section may also list systems without integration points, system upgrades that are not included, and anything else that someone might mistakenly assume is in scope.

If the team has generated a lot of out-of-scope ideas, consider capturing them in a separate document or parking lot so they're not lost. This section can create a lot of conversation—and it should! It will help the team stay on track as the project progresses.

Visual Models

Visuals often communicate more easily than words, and adding one or two visuals to your scope statement can support clarity and alignment. The following visual models are particularly useful during scope definition:

- **System context diagram.** A useful tool for confirming scope with business and technical stakeholders and ensuring that business analysis addresses all necessary integration requirements. The "Technique in Focus" section later in this chapter discusses system context diagrams in detail.
- **Data flow diagram.** Illustrates how information flows through, into, and out of a system. They are especially useful when evaluating data-intensive processes and looking at how data is shared between systems or organizations. Data flow diagrams show the data sources, data processes, and data stores.
- **High-level process model.** An intuitive way for stakeholders to understand the organization's fundamental processes, clarify how work gets done, and appreciate how value is

delivered. Most business analysts create simple workflow diagrams that show the end-to-end business process. These models are discussed in detail under "Technique in Focus" in chapter 2.

- **Use case diagram.** Useful on a project with many use cases to help the team see who is using the system and what functions users can execute. The diagram shows actors, use cases, and the relationships between them.
- **Wireframe/prototype.** A visual showing the possible look and feel of the user-facing system. (See chapter 6 for more details.)

Drafting one or more of these models and reviewing them with stakeholders can confirm everyone's understanding of the solution approach.

Get Buy-In on Scope

To achieve alignment and clarity, the business analyst must get buy-in on scope from both the business and technology teams. Creating a single scope document helps to facilitate this shared understanding. While everyone may not agree that the scope represents the best possible decisions, they should at least understand what the scope is and why those decisions were made.

The business analyst may need to review the scope statement multiple times, facilitate discussions with disagreeing parties, and negotiate trade-offs. Ultimately, the business sponsor makes the final decision, but the more buy-in exists now, the easier the rest of the change effort will be.

> ### *Enhance Your Productivity with Generative AI*
>
> - Generate a draft scope statement using the template and unstructured project information, such as meeting notes or transcripts.
> - Evaluate your scope statement for internal conflicts, inconsistent terminology, and other tweaks to improve clarity.

✅ Success Strategy: Confirm the Business Case

Before finalizing the scope statement, take a step back and evaluate whether the solution scope meets the business objectives and will deliver a positive ROI. It can be a tough pill to swallow after all this analysis, but sometimes the best solution approach possible within the constraints results in scope with a negative ROI.

Some organizations have a gate review in which an executive team reviews all projects before anyone does further planning. Many do not, and teams in those organizations sometimes forge ahead on initiatives that do not make sense.

Since business analysts are focused on business value, this is an area of potential growth and leadership. But be cautious about how you communicate your insights. Discuss your findings with your most trusted adviser first. Confirm that your analysis did not over-look potential benefits that weren't fully articulated. For example, sometimes the short-term ROI is negative but the organization is consciously investing in longer-term results that don't have clear metrics, such as brand recognition or the ease of doing business. Sometimes the change effort is part of a larger plan that isn't fully revealed to the team.

Canceling an initiative with a negative ROI is one option, but there are many other possibilities:

- Revise your business objectives to uncover additional value.
- Explore different solution approaches that require less investment.
- Cut scope to focus on the most valuable items that require the least investment.
- Put the initiative on hold until the return increases or more cost-effective solutions are available.
- Combine this initiative with related initiatives that can share solution costs, thereby reducing the overall investment dedicated to this initiative.

An initiative with a negative ROI or a return that is not as great as other possible choices siphons time, energy, and resources from other, more valuable initiatives. An organization that continues to invest in the wrong initiatives cannot thrive.

▶ Technique in Focus: System Content Diagrams

One of the most useful visual models to clarify scope, particularly for impacted business applications and system integrations, is the system context diagram.

A system context diagram shows how one system interfaces with other systems. It puts a primary system in context with other systems.

Figure 6. A system context diagram for a customer portal

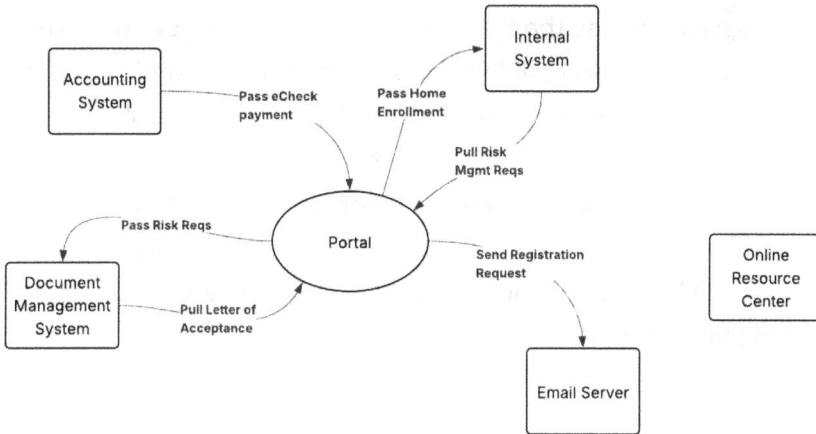

The system context diagram shown in figure 6 was created to show how a customer portal would interact with the other systems maintained by the organization. This model contains three key elements:

- **The core system** is represented by the oval in the middle of the diagram. Typically, a system context diagram only shows the data flows to and from one core system.
- **Integrated systems,** represented by rectangular boxes, that pass data to or from the core system. In this example, the Online Resource Center was an existing customer portal that would be retired, and thus has no integration line.
- **Integration lines** use arrows to show what information is passed between two systems and the direction of the data flow.

This is an example of a more detailed system context diagram; in addition to showing which systems were connected, it identified the types of interactions between the systems and the kinds of information being shared.

Another key element of this project was enabling customers to see information previously only available in the internal system. This diagram showed the full extent of information types that would and would not be accessible to customers and what kind of updates customers would be able to make so the team could establish the overall technical scope of the project.

This simple model can surface a lot of assumptions and constraints for technical integrations and show them to stakeholders in a way that is quickly understood. It's by far my favorite visual model to include in a scope statement.

❯❯ Next Steps

Scope becomes your guide through the rest of the Business Analysis Process steps. It also creates momentum for the change effort.

Here are some next steps to implement what you've learned:

- Identify potential types of solutions, including business process improvements and software capabilities.
- Identify the business and technical stakeholders to collaborate with on the solution approach and craft a plan for facilitating scope discussions.
- Prioritize the capabilities, to ensure that the highest-value business priorities receive the most attention from the team.
- Craft a scope statement and get buy-in from all key stakeholders.
- Confirm the business case, to keep the organization from investing resources in inconsequential projects.
- Experiment with creating a system context diagram to clarify system integration requirements.

With a clear understanding of scope, the target is clear and everyone should be able to see how they can contribute to a successful outcome.

4

Formulate Your Business Analysis Plan

When kicking off a live workshop or training program, I love to ask what challenges participants are experiencing in their work. Almost invariably, the most common one is unrealistic deadlines. Often, the deadline for the requirements is set before there is a clear scope, a team, or any understanding of what the business analyst needs to do to contribute to a successful outcome.

Business analysts operate in fast-paced, deadline-driven environments. Sometimes, *when* it needs to be done seems to matter more than *what* needs to be done. Whether you have a little time or a lot, you need solid planning skills to succeed. Planning your work and setting deadlines for yourself and your stakeholders will get you out of reactive mode and into proactively bringing your best to an initiative.

It's one thing to respond to an unrealistic deadline by simply saying it's not possible. It's another to provide a credible plan, offer trade-offs, and articulate the risks. Having a plan invites a completely different type of conversation, with the business analyst owning the narrative of what's possible and why certain activities take as long as they do. One program participant said this was how he stopped feeling like a ping-pong ball, bouncing from one bite-sized requirement to the next and freaking out when his manager asked for some sort of deliverable. Now, with this process, he keeps himself on track.

Still, many business analysts resist planning—often because they don't know how long their work will take. Here's a bit of tough love: To cultivate credibility and respect, you need to be able to plan your work, make a commitment, and follow through. Plus, planning the business analysis effort provides structure, so you actually know whether you are on track or need to course correct.

Analysis work can be difficult to plan. It's inherently collaborative, and depends on the participation and engagement of business and technology stakeholders. It's also inherently ambiguous. It involves exploring unknowns and peeling back layers. It's like working on an old house: You never know what you'll find when you pull up the floorboards or take down a wall!

While these are valid reasons to build cushion into your plan and discuss the risks, they aren't reasons to avoid planning. After all, developers and software testers have to plan and estimate their work. Why should we business analysts be any different?

The business analysis plan spells out the business analysis work to be completed, with the support of business and technical stakeholders. It is not the plan for the entire initiative. The business analysis plan answers the following questions:

- When will the business analysis effort be complete?
- What is everyone's role in the analysis process?
- How much time will be required from each stakeholder?
- What requirements analysis documents will be created and how will they support other team members?
- What should the business analyst work on and when?
- What sequence of deliverables will best minimize risk, maximize stakeholder time, and support the implementation team?

Figure 7 shows an example of a completed business analysis plan. By answering these questions, creating a formal business analysis plan, and reviewing it with the team, you can get stakeholder buy-in on their contributions, which minimizes the risk of them disengaging from the process.

Figure 7. A business analysis plan for a mobile insurance application

Deliverable Name	Estimated Effort	Duration	Start	End	Stakeholders	Assumptions/ Dependencies
Submit Claim (Process)	20 hours	4 weeks	1/5	2/2	Agent, Customer Rep	
Approve Claim (Process)	15 hours	3 weeks	2/5	2/23	Agent, Claims Rep	Submit Claim Process
Submit Claim (Use Case)	10 hours	2 weeks	2/26	3/9	Agent, Claims Rep, Tech Lead	Submit/Approve Claim Processes
Upload Supporting Documentation (Use Case)	10 hours	2 weeks	1/5	3/23	Agent, Customer Rep, Tech Lead	
Create Profile (Use Case)	10 hours	2 weeks	1/22	2/2	Agent, Customer Rep, Tech Lead	
Login to Mobile Application (Use Case)	10 hours	1 week	2/5	2/11	Customer Rep, Tech Lead	
Glossary	2 hours	n/a	1/5	ongoing	ALL	Completed throughout
Business Domain Model	8 hours	2 weeks	2/12	2/25	Agent, Rep, Claims Rep, Tech Lead	Glossary
Data Dictionary	15 hours	2 weeks	2/26	3/9	Agent, Customer Rep, Claims Rep, Tech Lead	
Data Map (to migrate data from existing claims system)	40 hours	4 weeks	2/12	4/8	Agent, Customer Rep, Claims Rep, Tech Lead	Data Dictionary

---

This business analysis plan template is available for download in the Business Analyst Success Pack.

Define the Deliverable Types

Putting a business analysis plan together is a bit like fitting together pieces of a puzzle, and at the same time cutting out the pieces and drawing the finished picture. You work through a few different lenses and perspectives and iterate until all the pieces fit and the outcome is acceptable.

The first piece to work through is which business analysis deliverables you need to create. There are two primary factors to consider: methodology and scope.

The methodology is the collection of existing decisions about how to approach the change effort. The Business Analysis Process is a component of the overall change delivery process, so the deliverables should fit with the larger methodology. Some organizations have a defined methodology, such as an agile software development process or an iterative software development process, which dictates many of the choices. In other cases, the team may be responsible for choosing the methodology. In either case, the deliverables the organization typically requires for a project are a good starting point.

If you've clarified the business analysis role and expectations as part of Step 1, "Get Oriented," you should have a sense of the expectations around deliverables. This is a great time to connect with your implementation stakeholders and ask them about any specific needs they foresee for the initiative or any specific types of documentation they'd prefer to receive.

From this input, create a preliminary list of the types of business analysis deliverables that would be valuable on this project. For example, on an agile team, the business analyst might be responsible for creating a product backlog and individual user stories for each item on the backlog. In an iterative environment, the plan might call for use cases and wireframes for each key feature. In either environment, business process documents or workflow diagrams might be necessary to define the future-state business processes.

The second consideration is the scope—specifically, the elements from the scope that need further detail for the business and technology teams to implement them successfully. The business analysis deliverables should provide the information needed to create detailed requirements and should ensure the scope is fully implementable.

Figure 8 lists the most common business analysis deliverables and the situations where they are most relevant and useful.

Figure 8. Common business analysis deliverables

Deliverable Type	Useful When ...	Methodology
Business Process Models: Current State or "As Is"	The existing business process is not well understood	Any
Business Process Models: Future or "To Be"	The project will result in changes to existing business processes or new business processes that need to be defined and implemented.	Any
Business Rules Spreadsheet or Database	There are multiple business rules that need to be maintained separately. Business rules can also be included in other documents, such as use cases, user stories, and functional requirements documents.	Any
Data Dictionary	New types of information need to be stored in a new or updated database structure.	Any
Data Map	Data needs to be migrated from one database to another or integrated between systems.	Any

Deliverable Type	Useful When ...	Methodology
Epic	Your team wants to break a large initiative into manageable chunks of scope. Epics are often decomposed into product backlogs and user stories, and several use cases may be written to decompose an epic into functional requirements.	Agile
Functional Requirements Document (FRD) or Software Requirements Specification (SRS)	Defining functional requirements in a single document for sharing or eventually capturing them in a requirements management tool.	Traditional
Nonfunctional Requirements List	Certain qualities of the software, such as performance, usability, and security are important. Like business rules, nonfunctional requirements may be included in other documents such as use cases, user stories, or a software requirements specification.	Any
Product Backlog	Working on an agile team, where the list of user stories is kept in a product backlog that the team uses to plan, prioritize, and sort ideas.	Agile
Training Guide	The end users will face significant changes or be expected to use new tools and/or follow new business processes when doing their work.	Any
Use Cases	Defining functional software requirements that are interactive in nature.	Any
User Acceptance Test Plans/Cases	The end users or business stakeholders are expected to be part of the effort to test and approve the functional requirements implemented as part of the software solution.	Any
User Interface Specification	Defining specific business rules for a user interface screen of a software application.	Any

Deliverable Type	Useful When ...	Methodology
User Stories	Capturing the details of specific item on the product backlog for implementation and testing.	Agile
Wireframes	Defining the flow or look of the user interface for a software application.	Any

This reference list is available for download in the Business Analyst Success Pack.

A few best practices can guide deliverable choices that support positive project outcomes. First, the most efficient use of business analysis effort is to choose business analysis deliverables that are both containers for the detailed requirements and valuable analysis tools. Examples include business process maps, use cases, and data models. In an agile environment, the business analysis plan may center on user stories, but user stories are often inadequate on their own. Producing additional deliverables encourages strong analytical thinking, reveals the big picture, and uncovers otherwise missed requirements.

Second, don't overlook the business side of the implementation. Even though the software aspect of the implementation typically requires more time and effort and is seen as the critical path project dependency, helping the business change ensures delivery of a positive ROI. Explore deliverables like training guides and future-state business processes to support the business in embracing the new processes and systems.

Finally, consider what deliverables you'll leave behind. Up-to-date system documentation can be extremely valuable as a reference and support future projects. So can deliverables like glossaries, business processes, use cases, and data models. Future-state documentation can often become current-state documentation once the initiative is complete. And each change effort provides an opportunity to analyze the process, functionality, and data around the changes and create a more comprehensive baseline.

Identify Specific Deliverables

For each deliverable type identified in the previous step, brainstorm a list of possible deliverables that will cover the scope. Often this can be a team activity, and it's a great way to include business and technical stakeholders in defining the business analysis plan.

For example, consider a business analyst on a project to help a nonprofit implement a new donor management system with the goal of streamlining donor communication, reducing redundant donor communication activities, and creating the potential to increase donations through improved outreach. The team has decided to constrain the scope to out-of-the-box functionality.

In identifying deliverable types, the business analyst determines that this will involve analyzing the current state of donor communication management, which uses spreadsheets and personal contact management systems. In addition, each individual's list of contacts will need to be migrated into the new central database and consolidated. Finally, once the new software is in place the business process will change, which requires future-state business process models. Since there will be no new functionality or system configurations, there are no new software requirements to model.

Here's a potential list of actual deliverables for this project:

Current-State Business Process Models
Manage Donor List
Communicate with Donor

Business Domain and Data Models
Glossary
Business Domain Model
Data Dictionary

Future-State Business Process Models
Manage Donor List (Updated)
Communicate with Donor (Updated)

After listing specific deliverables, refer to the scope statement to ensure the list fully details the scope.

- Are all impacted business processes and business areas included?
- Are all capabilities covered by functional or software requirements analysis techniques?
- Are all impacted systems accounted for?
- Are all data flows accounted for?
- Is there any supplemental documentation, like a glossary, that would make everything else easier?

At this point, you can add the specific deliverable names to your business analysis planning spreadsheet. Although you'll adjust this list often as you get into the details, you now have a starting place.

Deliverables are not just an output; they are part of the analysis process. Business analysts don't create a current-state business process model just so they can check it off a list. They create it to facilitate understanding of how the business stakeholders are completing a process today in order to help them improve that process and, in this scenario, transition it over to a new system. This should be the case with every deliverable. Whenever you add something to the list, ask yourself:

- Is this deliverable really necessary?
- What questions will this deliverable help me answer?
- Is this information covered elsewhere?
- What existing documentation can I leverage so I don't have to start from scratch?

These questions also apply to each section of a longer template your organization might use, like a business requirements document or functional specification. Treating the template like a checklist of items to consider in your business analysis effort rather than a mandate will help you be more effective and efficient as a business analyst.

Identify Stakeholders

Your list of deliverables will be the cornerstone of your planning, but by itself it doesn't say much about how the business analysis effort will unfold.

Consider each of the deliverables you've identified. Who needs to be involved to discover and analyze those requirements? For example, uncovering information about the current business process to close a lead will likely require involving the sales manager and one or more subject matter experts from the sales team. Identify each person by name. If there's a gap in your stakeholder list, identify the role and capture an open issue to identify the appropriate person.

Stakeholders can fill different roles in relation to project deliverables. Common stakeholder roles are:

- **Responsible** – those who do work to achieve the task, such as a business analyst
- **Accountable** – the person who ultimately owns the deliverable; often the sponsor or a manager-level

stakeholder representing an aspect of the change on
the sponsor's behalf
- **Consulted** – those whose opinions and input are solicited;
often subject matter experts representing all impacted
departments
- **Informed** – those who are updated on progress but not
directly involved, such as the project manager and/or
functional manager

Together these four roles form what's called the "RACI" matrix,
a standard way of evaluating the roles individuals can fill in relation
to a deliverable. Be aware that someone else on the team, such as
the project manager, product owner, or business sponsor, may be
performing similar analysis. Collaborate whenever you can!

Whether or not you use a RACI matrix, define who is responsible
for what when it comes to creating, reviewing, and validating a deliverable, and ensure everyone understands what's involved in fulfilling
their responsibilities. Make these commitments as concrete as possible
with your stakeholders. Share how many meetings you'd expect them
to attend and when. Identify what sorts of feedback or input they can
expect to be responsible for between meetings. Ask them whether
they anticipate having all the information they need or will need
to include additional stakeholders in their decision-making or information gathering processes, which could mean more work for them.
If possible, book workshops well in advance or schedule regular
sessions throughout the project so they have plenty of time to
prepare and bandwidth to participate effectively.

Be careful not to overlook the technology stakeholders who will
implement the solution. I remember meeting my original mentor
on my first project after I'd moved onto a new role in a new company.
We were talking about my current work, and I told her we'd finished

dozens of use cases, but I was still waiting for the contract to be signed with the technology implementation team.

"Then you aren't really done," she said. "You just have drafts."

I had been feeling good about my progress up to this point, but she was right! The business perspective is not enough. The technical perspective includes constraints and feasibility, ensuring your requirements are actually implementable.

While it often doesn't make sense to include technical stakeholders in every requirements-related discussion, involve them before the requirements are considered complete. Make sure there is a technical stakeholder for each software or data requirements deliverable. Collaborate to identify the best approach for when and how to get them involved in reviews before finalizing the requirements. As early as possible, identify technical specialists representing each system, and be sure to include developers, database engineers, testers, security engineers, network engineers, and architects. Having them on board with the requirements will be vital as the effort unfolds.

Estimate the Analysis Work

The next piece of the puzzle is estimating the analysis work. There are two elements to consider: the work to complete the deliverable, or estimated effort, and the time that will pass while creating the deliverable, or estimated duration.

Estimated effort is not the same as duration. The estimated effort is the actual time it will take to do the discovery, analysis, and validation work for a deliverable. A deliverable that requires 15 hours of effort may take two or three weeks (or more) to complete due to the time it takes to schedule interviews, locate documentation, balance commitments to multiple projects, and so on.

Making a reasonable estimate means thinking through how the requirements process might go. Consider the following buckets of work:

- How many meetings it will take to discover the information to complete an initial draft of the deliverable?
- How many drafts or iterations it will take to hash out a complete deliverable?
- How long it will take to make updates after each discussion?

I typically plan three hours of analysis work for every hour of meeting time. If it will take three one-hour meetings to discover information related to a deliverable and ultimately confirm the deliverable, that deliverable requires 12 hours of estimated effort (nine hours of analysis and documentation work and three hours of actual meeting time). The additional nine hours provide time for research, exploration, analysis, and identifying questions and gaps. As business analysts learn how to leverage generative AI to support drafting, reviewing, and researching tasks, independent analysis will probably require less time, leaving more time for collaboration.

Once you have a rough estimate, you may want to add time to account for other factors:

- your personal experience doing business analysis in general or this type of business analysis
- any time needed to get up to speed in this domain
- demanding stakeholders who may be difficult to engage, requiring you to use a variety of elicitation techniques or to prepare supplemental materials for review
- challenging stakeholder groups who tend to engage in a lot of back-and-forth and be difficult to align on the desired requirements
- unknowns or complexity about the requirements that may require extra time

With the estimated effort in hand, consider the duration for completing this deliverable. The number of requirements sessions is often a critical factor. If a deliverable will take 15 hours and three requirements sessions to create, will you be able to host all those sessions in one week? Often that will take two or three weeks at minimum.

The availability of stakeholders is another key factor. Understanding stakeholder commitments and calendars will help you determine reasonable task durations, and therefore deadlines.

On one project, my primary stakeholder and subject matter expert was only in the office two days a week and was sometimes busy with other work. I was lucky to get two one-hour meetings with her each week, and sometimes I had to make do with one. Originally, the project manager had expected me to be able to work without this stakeholder directly involved in every step, but this assumption did not prove out. Her availability significantly impacted the project duration, and we updated the timelines after working through the first few deliverables.

When considering durations, remember to factor in your other responsibilities: attending meetings, supporting other team members, working on other projects, and making general contributions to your business analysis team. Assuming that you will have a full work week for project-related activities leads to burnout and missed deadlines. Give yourself a set amount of buffer time for any non-project work and, if you are balancing multiple projects, allocate a specified number of hours each week to each initiative.

Sequence the Analysis Work and Create a Timeline

Now it's time to sequence the work. This is where the puzzle pieces really start to fit together—or, depending on the complexity and desired timeline, get really difficult to fit together.

With the estimated effort and duration calculated, look at the timelines for creating each deliverable and think about how to sequence them logically. There are several factors to consider: identifying dependencies, working to the project's critical path, reducing ambiguity and complexity, and generating quick wins.

Identify Dependencies

First, consider dependencies intrinsic to the business analysis plan. Obviously, you cannot create every deliverable at once. Some deliverables will be dependent on others, meaning they can't be started or finished until the dependent deliverable is complete. For example, you may not be able to determine your use case updates until you understand your current business processes.

Also consider stakeholder commitments—how much time they've said they can allocate to the requirements process. Be sure the plan doesn't exceed that commitment by assuming a stakeholder will work on multiple deliverables at the same time. Build in time for holidays and leave too, so they don't derail the timeline.

This is also a good time to identify any dependencies on other team members; for example, people you need to make a key technical decision (like signing a vendor or choosing a software system), confirm scope, or assign business stakeholders.

Work to the Critical Path

The next consideration is the initiative's critical path. Which deliverables will move the team forward the fastest? Try to eliminate bottlenecks by prioritizing requirements deliverables that enable the implementation team to start work sooner rather than later.

For example, if a specific set of use cases is scheduled to be implemented during the first iteration of the project, the business analyst would work on those use cases first, before the use cases scheduled for subsequent iterations. Or, in an agile environment, the business analyst would work on the user stories for the current or next sprint before tackling any other deliverables.

The plan for the mobile insurance application, shown in figure 7, assumes that work on some of the more generic use cases like uploading documents and creating profiles can run alongside the business process work. This compresses the overall timeline for business analysis.

Remember that as work progresses, the critical path changes. Deliverables that were not on the critical path in week 1 may be on the critical path in week 4. Review the plan regularly and adjust it to be sure the implementation team is getting the information they need.

Reduce Ambiguity and Complexity

Another common approach to sequencing requirements deliverables is focusing first on the deliverables with the most unknowns or the most risk. The goal is to discover information that will have the biggest potential impact as early as possible so the team can manage any associated risks or dependencies appropriately. Here are a few common areas of ambiguity or complexity:

- unknown business requirements
- potential for changing business requirements
- anticipated disagreement among stakeholders
- core features or business processes
- unknown or new solution/technology components
- features that drive the core technical architecture

To reduce ambiguity and complexity, evaluate each deliverable for unknowns and potential risks—both requirements-related risks and solution-related risks. Then collaborate with the business and implementation teams to sequence the deliverables so the biggest unknowns are discovered first. Teams that collaborate on their respective plans can often find opportunities to sequence deliverables in ways that reduce ambiguity and complexity while working to a shared critical path.

Often, reducing ambiguity and complexity will mean drafting several high-impact deliverables first and then circling back to them once the most important decisions are made. This work pattern tends to extend the business analysis timeline, but it can facilitate a shorter project timeline because it minimizes risks quickly.

An advantage to this approach is that it generates more relevant information early in the initiative, so the initiative will probably will run more smoothly and face less unexpected change. The disadvantage is that it can feel like the effort gets off to a slow start, which can reduce stakeholder engagement and buy-in. Showcase how the early analysis work lays out a solid foundation for project success. Consider making a comparison to construction: architects and builders invest substantial time in designs, permits, scheduling, and foundation work before starting on a house.

Generate Quick Wins

A final consideration when sequencing deliverables is generating quick wins. This is an especially viable option on agile teams where there are opportunities to complete multiple production releases within a single initiative. Implementing a set of relatively simple but high-impact requirements yields substantial value early and can generate buy-in that drives the rest of the effort forward. Another version of a quick win is discovering a business process change that can happen before the technology aspect of the solution is implemented. And even without an interim software release, you can cultivate the perception of quick wins by focusing on the deliverables with the highest perceived value to your stakeholders first.

Quick wins create engagement, especially from wary business stakeholders. This is especially useful on initiatives that require a culture change to be successful. But it's easy to lose sight of the big picture if you focus too much on quick wins, which could lead to discovering information that shifts the solution approach after key decisions have already been made.

Create a Timeline

All these approaches have their pros and cons. In most environments, you'll blend all approaches to sequence your requirements definition in the best possible way. And collaboration is key. Business analysis work does not happen in a vacuum. Effective analysts include perspectives from both business and technical stakeholders, and consider how the business analysis effort fits into the overall plan.

As the puzzle pieces begin to fit together, identify a reasonable target date for each deliverable that puts some pressure on you and your stakeholders to keep moving, but not so much pressure that you are behind from the beginning with no way to catch up.

Don't overanalyze the sequence of deliverables and neglect actually getting started. Invest a relatively small amount of time—no more than the time you'd invest in creating any single medium-sized deliverable on your list—in establishing a reasonable sequence. Review your plan with significant stakeholders to gain buy-in, so they know what to do to ensure the business analysis effort is successful.

Then get started.

As new information surfaces, you can always revise your plan and work sequence accordingly.

Enhance Your Productivity with Generative AI

- Identify the types of business analysis deliverables for your scope and methodology.
- Identify specific business analysis deliverables to cover your scope.
- Provide criteria or baseline data from similar projects and ask for business analysis estimates.
- Ask for sequencing options based on criteria such as stakeholder availability, risk, and priorities.
- Provide your deliverables, estimates, durations, and dependencies, and a start date, and ask AI to assign dates.
- Review your plan and identify gaps.

✓ Success Strategy: Collaborate Well with an Agile Software Development Team

Before we move on to discovering, analyzing, and validating the detailed requirements, let's review how planning fits into an agile software development context.

A key agile value is responding to change over following a plan. While it can be tempting to take this as permission to skip all kinds of planning, the reality is that a lot of planning goes into getting an agile team into a productive and efficient flow of activity. Responding to change over following to a plan means that you don't allow the plan to become fixed and constrain the team from responding to necessary change. Planning the business analysis effort is not incompatible with agile practices. Your planning can and will support the effectiveness of the entire software development team.

Agile is a set of organizing principles for developing software, but it's not a business analysis process. The scope of the business analysis effort includes collaborating with the technical team to support the implementation of working software, but it also supports the business stakeholders in navigating change and gaining alignment across multiple departments and stakeholders about desired outcomes.

High-performing technology teams are aware that business stakeholders need more time and focus to ensure the software they are asking for solves the right problem. Business stakeholders also need help updating the business process to leverage new software capabilities. A lot of this work needs to happen either outside the sprint or before it.

Here are some of the questions an agile business analyst will want to answer while planning the business analysis effort:

- How long will the sprints be?
- What happens inside a sprint? Is there time for elicitation and requirements work, or is the sprint all about developing and testing?
- What is the desired outcome of a sprint? Is it production-ready code? What does that mean? What is the "definition of done" and how does the business analyst support this?
- How does the team decide what to work on inside a sprint?
- What state does a product backlog need to be in before a sprint?
- What state do the user stories need to be in before a sprint?
- Who is responsible for the product backlog and user stories? (While these are natural responsibilities for an agile business analyst to take on, your team may have a different way of doing things.)
- What requirements work, if any, will happen inside the sprint?

The goal is to figure out exactly how to fit the detailed functional requirements work into the software development team's agile process.

One common way to complete a business analysis plan on an agile team is to work one or two sprints ahead of the development team, and potentially much further ahead on areas that require significant business process realignment. This is one way to work to the critical path. To do this, prioritize the next set of product backlog items, then identify any business analysis deliverables and stakeholder involvement required to clarify the details of those product backlog items so they are ready when the associated sprint begins.

However you decide to move forward, remember that agile teams will benefit from a business analysis structure and plan.

⏩ Next Steps

The business analysis plan is a useful tool for cultivating alignment around the business analysis role and deliverables. A careful plan will ensure you are as effective as possible and focused on the work that really matters. This is not about overplanning; it's about optimizing your time and the time investment from your stakeholders within both the business and technology teams.

Here are some next steps to implement what you've learned:

- Define the types of business analysis deliverables you need to create to integrate into the software development methodology.
- Identify the specific business analysis deliverables that will fully detail out the scope.
- Identify the stakeholders who need to be involved in each deliverable and ensuring they are ready to engage.

- Estimate the effort and duration of the business analysis work.
- Sequence the business analysis work effort to minimize effort and risk while supporting the other members of the team and the overall plan.

5

Define Detailed Requirements

One of my guilty pleasures is asking the question that makes everyone pause, knowing that it's an important question yet not knowing the answer. It can be a bit uncomfortable to hold the pause. People can get a bit squirmy in the not-knowing. But there is also a sense of recognition that "this person just saw something all the rest of us would have missed." It inspires respect and credibility and demonstrates the often-unseen value of business analysis in a palpable way.

One day I was working with Vicki, a smart, strategic sales leader who thought through possibilities in such detail that analyzing requirements for her projects was almost boring. As we worked through a complex set of requirements, I asked a question that made Vicki pause. I had anticipated a requirement that she hadn't. I can't remember the question, or even much about the project, but I remember the moment and the feeling vividly—the sense that for all Vicki's foresight I was bringing my own analysis and understanding to the table, and I had earned a new level of credibility and respect.

Thinking of this requirement and asking this question wasn't a magic trick. It came from a disciplined process of discovery, analysis, and validation—the work to define the detailed requirements.

Defining the requirements is often the most visible work business analysts do. It requires most of the effort, and stakeholders often want this work started as quickly as possible. The goal is to make the scope implementable—to give the team all the context and information they need to create the solution. Requirements that are clear, concise, and actionable, that balance business outcomes with initiative and technology constraints, make this possible. Without them, implementation teams often flounder and fail to connect the dots in a way that delivers on the original business case.

This chapter discusses three key stages in defining requirements: discovering information; analyzing the information and drafting requirements; and reviewing, validating, and finalizing the deliverables (see figure 9). This process focuses your efforts and puts you in a position to ask powerful questions. You can think through the requirements, ensuring no stone is unturned, even as you guide the team to identify the specific requirements and stay within scope.

Figure 9. A simple process flow for defining detailed requirements

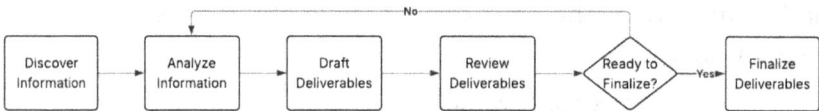

You'll go through the activities in this chapter for each deliverable identified in the business analysis plan, involving the right stakeholders at the right time, balancing business outcomes with constraints, and ultimately building engagement and gaining buy-in from all stakeholders on the actual, implementable changes that will be made. Alignment and buy-in from both business and technical stakeholders minimizes unnecessary rework and requirements churn. Ultimately, the goal of Step 5 is for each deliverable to be final, ready for the next step.

What the next step is will depend heavily on your role and the type of initiative. Be sure to know who does what based on the detailed requirements deliverables you define. This information will guide you in finalizing the deliverable and ensuring that you analyze information to the appropriate level, without being too vague and abstract or going too far into details that will be handled by other team members. If you don't know who is doing what with the requirements, now is the time to get that clarity by checking in with your technical team.

If the deliverables in this step will specify requirements for a technical solution, "final" typically means that the deliverable is ready for technical design and implementation and will support the creation of test cases. For deliverables that specify a business process change, "final" typically means sufficient to start a business change effort, which may involve deploying the new process, training existing staff, and updating training documentation for future new staff.

The groundwork in Steps 1 through 4 is designed to make this work as effective, efficient, and productive as possible. It's all necessary. Without a clear understanding of the business objectives, alignment around scope, and an intentional business analysis plan, you'll spend more time in Step 5 than you need to, experience more frustrations than necessary, and find yourself backtracking. But with a solid foundation, you can be the one who asks the savvy questions, even if you understand the least about the business, the technology, or both.

Stage 1 – Discover Information

The first stage in detailing the requirements is discovering the information needed to create a first deliverable draft or to take the next analysis step for each deliverable in your business analysis plan. You may face resistance to the need for additional discovery. A common misconception is that discovery happens early in the effort, before and during the scope definition phase, and then stops. In reality, discovery happens throughout the business analysis lifecycle. We are constantly learning new information and integrating it into our approach and the requirements. At this stage, we are building on the initial discovery work to discover business objectives and define scope, and getting into the more granular details of what the solution needs to do.

Here are some common elicitation techniques that work well for discovering information related to the detailed requirements, although not every deliverable requires every technique. I covered these techniques in chapter 2; I'm revisiting them again here with guidance on how to apply these techniques as part of defining specific, detailed requirements.

Document Analysis

Document analysis involves actively reading a document such as a regulation, a standard, a competitive product review, or customer suggestion logs—any source of information about what a customer might want, what a business user might need, or what changes might be mandated.

This is a great way to discover rules, possible requirements, and potential changes. It's also a great way to prepare for other techniques. Before interviewing a stakeholder, try to review current-state process documentation, training materials, and perhaps even the software used to complete the process.

One project I worked on involved building a web-based software application to collect information that customers had previously submitted using paper forms. I spent a significant amount of time reviewing those forms, reconciling the data elements across forms, and building a consolidated list of data elements in a spreadsheet. Document analysis enabled me to move the project and my own understanding forward even with the challenge of minimal stakeholder availability.

Today, generative AI tools can augment human document analysis by summarizing documents, pulling out salient points, or proposing a set of requirements. This can significantly streamline a time-intensive task.

A related technique is interface analysis, which involves gaining an understanding of a software system by exploring it. In a test environment, this might mean testing multiple paths through the system and exploring how it supports the business process.

Both document analysis and interface analysis allow you to work independently and avoid asking questions that have been answered, or are easy to answer, in the existing system. To use the previous example, asking stakeholders to list the data elements on forms for me would have wasted their time. Thanks to thorough document analysis, I could ask clarifying questions to reconcile inconsistent labels, identify the information required on each form, and focus on the workflows initiated when the forms were received.

There is a risk, though. Documentation is often inaccurate or outdated and may not represent stakeholders' perspectives. In the case of those forms, due to limited stakeholder availability, I spent a lot of time trying to reconcile data elements with slightly different labels across the forms and piecing together how those labels connected to the data elements in the business application. When I reviewed this with stakeholders, I found many of these inconsistencies were due to outdated naming conventions and obsolete data elements. Always validate the information gleaned from document and interface analysis with stakeholders, and be careful not to spend too much time on this activity.

Interviews

Interviews are one of the most common elicitation techniques. Interviews are often one-on-one, but they can also be done in a small group setting as long as you're careful to engage each participant and ensure they have the opportunity to share their perspective.

Preparation is key for interviews. Before the meeting, you want to develop an agenda and share it with all participants. It's also a good idea to develop a requirements questionnaire or a list of questions you intend to ask during the meeting.

While it may seem counterintuitive, one of the most notable communication skills you can develop is active listening. Listening involves the act of hearing at its most basic, physical level, but is really about understanding what the person talking to you is trying to communicate. Active listening also involves asking relevant follow-up questions until you develop a shared understanding.

You can practice this as you go about your day, at work or home, by actively paraphrasing what you hear. When someone speaks to you, take a moment to reflect what you heard by paraphrasing it. They will tell you whether you got it right. Active listening and para-phrasing ensures understanding throughout a conversation and can clarify misunderstandings before they escalate.

Asking powerful questions is another key skill to cultivate. The ability to provoke real conversation—and where necessary, maybe even a bit of debate—helps get beneath the stated requirements to the real needs and outcomes. Asking open-ended questions (without yes or no answers) encourages creative responses. Some of the best questions bring about completely unexpected and tangential answers, surfacing information that you would not have thought to ask for. Unexpected information is a great outcome and a powerful indicator that you are digging into the most relevant details. Crafting a requirements questionnaire is a great first step to set yourself up for this kind of success.

▶ Technique in Focus: Requirements Questionnaires

A thorough requirements questionnaire will help ensure that you engage your stakeholders and streamline your discovery process. One participant reported eliminating several follow-up meetings by using our requirements questionnaire checklists along with active listening techniques.

When creating a requirements questionnaire, work through each feature or deliverable, one at a time. Write down what you know about that feature (or what you assume to be true about that feature), then start drafting questions. Most of the time, the questions evolve naturally as you think through the implications of a feature, but sometimes you'll need to spur your thinking a bit. Like a good story, detailed requirements will answer all the key questions: how, where, when, who, what, and why.

Here are some questions to stimulate your thinking.

How questions
- How will your stakeholders use this feature?
- Is this feature a process and, if so, what are the steps? Or, what questions can I ask to ascertain the steps?
- How might we meet this business need?
- How might we think about this feature a bit differently?
- How will we know this is complete? Or, what are the success criteria?

Where questions
- Where does the process start?
- Where would the user access this feature?
- Where would the user be located physically when using this feature? Are they at home? In the office? Off-site?
- Where would the results be visible?

When questions

- When will this feature be used?
- When do you need to know about ...?
- When will the feature fail?
- When will we be ready to start?
- When does this need to be completed?

Who questions

- Who will use this feature?
- Who will deliver the inputs for the feature?
- Who will receive the outputs of the feature?
- Who will learn about the results of someone using this feature?
- Who can I ask to learn more about this?
- Who can or cannot access this feature or information?

What questions

- What do I know about this feature? Or, what assumptions am I making about this feature that I need to confirm?
- What does this feature need to do?
- What is the result of doing this?
- What are the pieces of this feature?
- What needs to happen next?
- What must happen before?
- What if ...? (Think of all the alternative scenarios and ask questions about what should happen if those scenarios are true.)
- What needs to be tracked?
- What device will someone be using when they access this feature?
- What other questions should I be asking? (This is always a good one for yielding unexpected answers!)

Why questions

Why questions are great wrap-up questions because they help confirm that the requirements you just elicited map back to a need you identified when you scoped the project.

- Is there any other way to accomplish this?
- Does this feature meet the business need and solve the problem we're trying to solve?
- When we implement this feature, what will be true?
- What's the most important thing about this feature?

You'll notice that these why questions don't use the word *why.* Even though "why?" might be one of the most important business analysis questions, it can feel confrontational, so be sure to ask it with finesse.

One word of warning: The last thing you want to do here is run down your list of questions one by one. That can be a big waste of time and often doesn't lead to an engaging discussion. Instead, select a few core questions to get the stakeholder talking. Then, as they are talking about their vision for the feature, use your questionnaire to guide the conversation and ensure you don't miss anything.

If you aren't sure whether a question was answered, you can always rephrase it as "Is there anything else you want to share about {insert original question here}?" or "Did we cover everything related to {for example, how this process starts}?"

Enhance Your Productivity with Generative AI

- Share context about your initiative or feature and request a set of questions to ask.
- Share a set of questions from this list and ask for questions specific to your initiative, feature, or deliverable.
- Share the questions you've identified and generate additional questions to consider.

✔ Success Strategy: Ask the So-Called Stupid Question

Part of asking questions is sometimes being able to ask the so-called stupid question. Teachers often tell students that if one person has a question, others do too. I've found this to be true in my career as well. For example, in my first project we were discussing a design issue and everybody seemed to agree about the resolution. I thought one piece didn't quite make sense, but it was my first project and I trusted that the team knew better than I did. Three or four weeks later, the issue behind my "stupid" question came up and we ended up having to solve it later—at additional cost.

It can be difficult to ask these questions because sometimes people will think they really are foolish. Business analysts need a thick skin and the ability to ask the question and expect a response, as well as to put up with some negative nonverbal feedback when you start down that path.

At the beginning of this chapter I told you how I astonished Vicki with a "magic" question that caught her off guard. Dozens of times before that I had asked questions that she had ready answers to and clarified information she felt she'd already shared. She was too polite to be rude, but I could sense a bit of frustration from time to time. Yet asking those seemingly obvious questions led to the one that made her pause. You'll never get to the magic questions if you silence your doubts.

Still, you need to read the room. Sometimes there are other ways to get your questions answered, and sometimes you've pushed a specific stakeholder or group too far and they disengage. Get to the heart of issue by calling attention to stakeholder behaviors and requesting feedback on the communication process.

Sometimes stakeholders simply don't know the answers. That's when observation can create breakthroughs that interviews don't.

Observation

Observation involves watching someone complete a task or go through their typical work day. It's a great way to understand the current state of a business process and system functionality so you can start identifying opportunities for improvement. It's also a great technique to uncover nuances, exceptions, and missing connections between systems.

When observing, ask the person to explain their work as they go along, and ask follow-up questions to clarify what they are doing, why they are doing it, and how what they are doing impacts others. As you ask follow-up questions, you are looking to understand the end-to-end process, the handoffs, the business rules for each step, and the capabilities and limitations of the software. You may need to walk through the process a few times with a few different work items to fully understand it and flesh out all the nuances. With each subsequent walk-through, the process should get clearer and the discussion more focused.

The goal of document analysis, interviews, and observation is to elicit enough information to create a first draft of a deliverable that you can review and validate with stakeholders and that reflects your understanding back to them.

Stage 2 – Analyze Information and Draft Deliverables

Once you've uncovered the available information, it's time to prepare draft deliverables. Writing, visual modeling, and most types of deliverables create clarity. Preparing a deliverable isn't just organizing the information you've discovered. It's analyzing it and identifying more questions, cultivating a more complete representation of what the business wants. Deliverables can help you create positive momentum and keep your meetings on track.

Here are some ways to go about preparing draft deliverables:

- Use the information you've discovered to draft a deliverable.
- Use the structure of the document to identify assumptions to validate and gaps in understanding. This is where the analysis happens.
- Identify additional questions to ask your stakeholders. Consider embedding questions right in the draft deliverable. This makes it clear that there are open issues and that stakeholder involvement is key to progress.
- Accompany any text models with a visual. Prototypes and wireframes, covered in chapter 6, are particularly useful in helping stakeholders envision possible solutions.

Once you have prepared the first draft of the deliverable, which may be very rough and have several open issues, review it with stakeholders and to get critical input to ensure it is clear and complete.

A lot of business analysts focus on a specific set of deliverables as their primary output, but deliverables are not the goal of business analysis. Clarity and alignment are the goals. That means helping the business stakeholders get clear on what they want, ensuring their vision is complete at a detailed level and represents a desired understanding of the solution, and then communicating this to the implementation team. Deliverables certainly serve this purpose and play an important role in maintaining organizational knowledge, but deliverables themselves do not create understanding. That's why iterations and reviews are critical. Chapters 6 and 7 go into more detail about specific techniques and deliverables that can be used to model software and data requirements.

Stage 3 – Review, Validate, and Finalize Deliverables

With the deliverable drafted, it's time review, validate, and ultimately finalize the deliverables with appropriate business and technology stakeholders. This may take more than one round of review and validation. Drafting the deliverables uncovers information gaps; reviewing and validating deliverables helps uncover more information to fill those gaps. Further analysis based on the new information may generate more questions, and so the cycle continues until the team is ready to finalize the requirements for implementation.

Even in a fast-paced or agile environment, it's important to get to the right level of detail and rigor before implementation work begins. While agile practices allow more room for change, in my experience agile teams aren't too excited to make *unnecessary* changes.

On my first agile team, I was under a tight deadline heading into sprint 1 and I didn't have time to confirm the requirements with a key stakeholder. Going into the sprint, I presented my best guess, noting that I was making some assumptions. Just three days into a two-week sprint, I met with the stakeholder and had a set of changes; the development team asked to continue with the original requirements and make the adjustments in the next sprint. They were quite frustrated when we met to discuss sprint 2 and they had to rework more than half of what they had accomplished!

After that, I took a stronger position about validating the requirements before they were ready for a sprint.

Sometimes, the business stakeholders resist being involved in this part of the process. From their perspective, they provided a lot of information during the initial discovery and they've done all they need to do.

This is one reason to manage expectations. Try to end each discovery meeting by letting the stakeholders know that there could be more questions after the initial analysis. Also share that you want to be sure to capture exactly what they expect, so you'll need them to review the draft deliverables.

If stakeholders do resist, connect their involvement to progress toward their desired outcome. Instead of asking "Can we get to together to review these requirements?" say "Let's review these requirements and get them ready for implementation" or "Until we review and validate these requirements, the implementation team is on hold, and we run the risk of delaying the project."

To review and validate a deliverable, you will:

- ensure the requirements are clear and complete,
- get answers to all your questions,
- incorporate any new information into the deliverable,
- confirm that the requirements capture what the business wants the solution to do,
- align all impacted business stakeholders around the intended solution, and finally
- ensure the requirements are feasible within the technical constraints.

A simple deliverable may only need a single review cycle to answer a few simple questions. For a complex deliverable, you may go through several review cycles and revise your drafts heavily in between cycles.

One way to boost engagement during this process is to carefully consider who you involve. It's tempting to invite every project stakeholder to every meeting, but it's more effective to identify the people to be involved to discuss the open questions and move the deliverable forward. This can be tricky when you are new to the team. It's often best to start with a smaller set of primary business stakeholders and ask them who else should be involved.

It's also a good idea to loop in a primary technical stakeholder to understand the technical possibilities. Some technical experts will want to take part in the initial discussions to hear the perspectives of the stakeholders directly. Others prefer to wait until the initial discovery work is complete and the requirements are closer to final. When involving technical stakeholders early in an initiative, be sure they are prepared to listen and will not take ownership or try to get too specific about the solution details too early in the discovery process.

Questions may come up that require expertise from different areas of the organization. Address these questions in separate meetings or individual discussions. Then, as the business requests are close to complete, conduct a final deliverable review involving the implementation stakeholders and all other impacted business stakeholders.

Do not be tempted to try review and validation by email. Working meetings, whether in person or virtual, are a much better way to ensure shared understanding. When you sit down to review a requirements specification in a meeting, you know that people are reading it. The resulting discussions can help discover new requirements before they become costly late changes. Besides, a review meeting cultivates a certain accountability—as long as you ask your stakeholders to look you in the eye and confirm they are ready to take the next step.

Remember, while the business analyst drives the process to create, review, and finalize deliverables, the business analyst does not *own* the deliverable. Look back through the set of responsibilities in this section: Each one involves getting input and buy-in from the business stakeholders.

It's critically important that the business stakeholders feel ownership of the requirements when the deliverable is complete. They should understand the content, approve of the requirements, and feel that the requirements express what they want out of the solution. Without this level of buy-in, you risk implementing a solution that the business stakeholders see as a failure. If you are ready to finalize a deliverable but find that one or more stakeholders are not buying in, back up and either elicit more information from that stakeholder or conduct additional review cycles until buy-in is achieved.

There will be scenarios where the business's desired requirements or vision for the solution are not feasible within the project constraints. For example, one of my participants was working on a complex product setup and renewal process. There were many ways to accomplish the business objectives, but the way the business originally thought about the solution created unnecessary complexity or was actually not feasible. She recast the original requirements in new ways and gained buy-in on these alternate solutions before passing them along to the implementation team. As a result, the system was streamlined and the overall implementation effort was reduced.

Upon hearing the challenges she was facing, another participant eloquently articulated that her experience showcased how understanding *why* and not just precisely *what* the stakeholders think they want is so critical. When a requirement proves infeasible, explore alternative solutions that meet the underlying business needs and evaluate trade-offs. Negotiation is almost always required.

All this review and validation work happens in a series of working meetings—a technique that's relevant throughout the change effort. The following "Technique in Focus" section explains how to facilitate effective working that engage stakeholders and build project momentum.

Enhance Your Productivity with Generative AI

- Request drafts of any kind of deliverable to use as a starting point. Uploading a template for AI to use as an example, such as one of those included in the Business Analyst Success Pack, can improve the result.
- Upload your deliverable draft and ask for critiques, questions, and alternate scenarios to consider.
- Ask for ideas to work around a perceived technical constraint.
- Connect meeting transcripts and request summaries, action items, and updated deliverables.

▶ Technique in Focus: Facilitate Working Meetings

Working meetings are not status meetings, stand-ups, or team gatherings. They are true working sessions: collaborative and deliverable-focused. And they move the initiative forward.

Working meetings can happen virtually or in person.[7] Typically, they last 30–90 minutes; longer half-day and full-day sessions would be considered workshops. Much of the advice in this section applies to workshops as well, although they need even more preparation and structure.[8]

Most meetings you facilitate should be either working meetings or workshops. I like to put working meetings in the context of a milestone the team is working toward. This goes a long way toward

---

[7] For an in-depth exploration of strategies for virtual teams, see Penny Pullan, *Virtual Leadership: Practical Strategies for Success with Remote or Hybrid Work and Teams* (Kogan Page, 2022).

[8] A classic resource on workshops is Ellen Gottesdiener's *Requirements by Collaboration: Workshops for Defining Needs* (Addison-Wesley, 2002).

increasing stakeholder engagement, because the people you invite to your meetings will start to expect real work and decision-making.

There is an art and a science to facilitating working meetings. This section addresses three essential activities: preparation, facilitation, and wrap up.

Preparation

First, clarify the purpose of the meeting. What do you hope to accomplish? How will this meeting move this initiative forward? Here are a few examples:

- discover information related to a specific deliverable
- review or validate a specific deliverable, such as a business process, use case, or user story
- get input related to the scope, such as identifying the business objectives, brainstorming impacts to other systems and processes, or identifying capabilities to solve for the desired outcome
- assess the feasibility of a specific process or requirement
- analyze the impacts of a specific requirement or process

Avoid a purpose like "discuss a topic," as this isn't specific or goal-oriented. Be clear about what type of information the meeting will discover or what decisions the team needs to make. This is what makes it a working meeting rather than an open-ended discussion.

With the goal in mind, begin active meeting preparation:

- **Perform research.** What background information can you discover ahead of the meeting? Could you explore a system, review documentation, or meet with a subject matter expert to get some background?
- **Invite the right participants.** Who is needed to achieve the purpose of the meeting? Who might be interested? Keep

your attendee list to the minimum required to achieve the goal.

- **Craft an agenda.** Be clear about the purpose and then list the activities and discussions that attendees will participate in to get there.
- **Prepare documentation.** What can you prepare ahead of time to keep the meeting on track? For a discovery meeting, this could be a requirements questionnaire. For detailed requirements meetings, provide draft or near-final deliverables for review and feedback.
- **Reserve resources.** Make sure you have everything you need to succeed. Book a meeting room and any necessary equipment for an in-person meeting, or set up a virtual session for a remote meeting.
- **Ask for support.** Some working meetings can benefit from extra support, such as a dedicated notetaker or timekeeper. This can be a great opportunity to offer an aspiring business analyst, as it will let them observe business analysis discussions and practice listening and facilitation.

Enable stakeholders to prepare as well. Before the meeting, send the agenda and any documentation that you'd like people to review. Although many stakeholders will not review the documentation, your more introverted stakeholders will appreciate the opportunity.

Sending the agenda in advance and inviting feedback or dialogue can also surface relevant background information, or even a missed stakeholder. Loading your draft deliverable into a virtual whiteboard tool and asking participants to add sticky notes with their ideas or feedback is another great way to generate input before the meeting.

Facilitation

Once everything and everyone is in place, it's time to facilitate the meeting.

- **Get in the right mindset.** Whenever possible, spend 10 or 15 minutes before the meeting reviewing your notes, questions, agenda, and any deliverables. If you find yourself in back-to-back meetings, take a moment to ground yourself in the outcome of the working meeting before starting.
- **Introduce participants.** Unless all attendees know each other and have worked together recently, ask for short introductions. Share why each person is there and how they will contribute to the purpose of the meeting. This goes a long way toward managing the discussion before it even starts.
- **Review the meeting purpose and agenda.** Remind everyone of the meeting purpose and situate the meeting in the context of the initiative. For example: "Today we're going to do a final review of this use case. Once we've finalized it, the implementation team will begin design and development work." This can also be a great time to recap the status of the business analysis effort and what's happened so far thanks to their time and input.
- **Work through the agenda.** Use your prepared questions to start the conversation if needed, and refer to your questions before switching topics to ensure you've covered everything. Make sure to actively check on anyone who hasn't participated and ask them if they have anything to add. Remember to use active listening techniques to build trust and ensure understanding.
- **Capture notes.** If you are capturing notes electronically, be sure to mention this so people don't perceive your

typing as distraction. Better yet, share your notes on screen, update the deliverable in real time, or draw a model representing your understanding. These are all great ways to help everyone absorb the information that's being shared. Leveraging AI-generated summaries or transcripts can enable you to be more present in the meeting without the distraction of note-taking.

- **Clarify terms and ask follow-up questions.** The goal of a working meeting is to create a shared understanding and make decisions that move the project forward. If you don't understand something, it's likely that someone else is also unclear. Because recording tools are so prevalent now, facilitators sometimes rely on the recording instead of asking more questions. But questions clarify the discussion for everyone, and often the recording does not provide the clarity you expect, meaning you'll have to circle back around later.

- **Summarize discussions for participants.** Each time you move to the next agenda item, summarize the previous discussion, the decision, and any next steps. For example: "We discussed a lot of ideas for the registration process and decided to look at the feasibility of three different ideas. The next step is for me to bring these ideas to the implementation team." These pauses are also opportunities to confirm your understanding and can also help AI capture better recaps.

Some of these tips may seem counterintuitive given the fast pace of so many conversations today. These strategies require a slower pace and more squirmy pauses. Allowing for intentional pauses gives people time to think and connect ideas, and embracing the pause can be a game changer for your meeting facilitation. Build in pauses and give everyone a moment to understand and reflect. Stop to take a note or think through the implication of the information someone just shared. We too often overlook the value of the slowing down.

All business analysts will face challenging working meetings at some point. Even with the best preparation and the best of intentions, attendees will sometimes derail meetings with unrelated topics or disruptive behaviors. One minute you are having a productive conversation about a decision, and the next that decision has started an entirely different conversation. Sometimes it can be difficult to tell at first, because you may not have the same level of detailed knowledge about the business and system impacts. What might initially seem relevant often is not. Here's a way to interject if you're not sure:

> *I just want to step in for a moment. We're here today to discuss {meeting purpose/agenda item}. This might be relevant to making that decision, but I'm not making the connection. Could you please clarify? Have we gone off track?*

If you're certain the conversation is off track, here's one way to redirect:

> *I can see how that is important, and I understand that you need some time to talk about it. But if we don't talk about {this agenda item} now, I won't have this deliverable ready in time for the development team (or "... I'm concerned that we might slip on this piece of the project").*
>
> *Let's stay focused on {this agenda item}, just for this discussion, and I can schedule some time later to make sure that we discuss this other piece.*

Another challenge is when a necessary stakeholder doesn't show up. While it may be possible to tackle some agenda items, resist the temptation to have a discussion or make a decision that requires an absent person's input. This wastes everyone's time. It is often better to reschedule the meeting.

You can face a lot of pressure when canceling a meeting, and that pressure may tempt you to push forward without a key person. However, this is an opportunity to set the stage and establish clear boundaries. I've found that when I cancel a meeting due to non-engagement or nonparticipation, the right people start to show up to my meetings more often and come more prepared. Managing the short-term pressure has a lot of long-term benefits.

In one extreme example, I was working with a development manager who was going through some difficult personal issues and started to become uncharacteristically disruptive in meetings. He would actively change the topic, start a side conversation, or just start talking about something personal. I redirected him several times over the course of a few meetings, but the behavior didn't change. I finally told him that if he couldn't keep his contributions on topic, I would have to ask him to leave the meeting. It was wicked uncomfortable, but it worked.

The standards you set for communication and engagement demonstrate that you value your time and the time of everyone involved. Yes, we want to be proactive, to keep our stakeholders engaged, and to do everything we can to support them and their decision-making. We need to be flexible, but we're not powerless. Our time and contributions are also valuable, as are those of everyone else on the team. Taking strategic opportunities to establish clear expectations sets you up for long-term success.

Wrap Up

Wrapping up a meeting is a final opportunity to summarize what you've accomplished and get people excited about the requirements process. We want people to continue to invest their best efforts in our meetings. The more they feel like they accomplished something meaningful, the easier it will be to keep them engaged.

Leave a few minutes at the end of the meeting to recap the discussion, summarize next steps and action items, and connect this meeting to forward progress on the initiative. Most importantly, summarize specifically what the attendees will receive from you next based on the work done in the meeting, such as meeting notes or updated deliverables. Also identify action items assigned to any other attendees.

After the meeting, plan time to do the following:

- process new information
- update deliverables
- identify gaps and questions
- communicate action items for yourself and others
- share your progress with the team

This is when you follow through and make the discussion actionable. Have a strategy that works for your thinking style and analysis process. Historically, my practice was to type up detailed notes from my handwritten meeting notes, including additional information that surfaced as I was typing. Then I'd shift quickly to updating deliverables, prioritizing this work as soon as possible after the meeting ended. I'd send out my notes, with action items identified in the body of the email, and start preparing for the next meeting.

Today, we can leverage recordings and AI to summarize meeting transcripts, draft detailed notes, list action items, and even make updates to deliverables. Remember to critically examine what AI generates and ensure that it accurately represents the discussion. Eventually we should see integrated toolsets that handle the follow-up communication and integrate with our requirements and project management tools. It took me a long time to make the shift to generative AI because writing is how I think. Over time I learned how to use it to make leaps in progress without losing my connection with the thread of analysis and decision-making. As you experiment with new tools, make sure you use them in a way that supports your thinking and analysis process.

✅ Success Strategy: Prevent Scope Creep

While eliciting information, creating draft deliverables, and finalizing those deliverables, some business analysts get so involved with the possibilities and the potential problems to be solved that they identify a lot more detailed requirements. It is easy to get caught up in the details of the requirements and unconsciously allow the scope to expand.

Allowing scope creep and adding complexity is human nature. I'll share a personal example: When I was buying new shoes for a trip to Disney World, the saleswoman talked me into special socks fitted to the right and left foot. It sounded great in principle, but half the time I put them on the wrong feet. Often I didn't notice this until after I got my first shoe on, which meant a lot of extra work to switch my socks. Perhaps if I were running at an elite level the extra complexity would be worth it, but even after 20,000 steps each day around Disney World, I didn't notice any difference.

On software initiatives, scope creep tends to happen inside specific requirements deliverables and while specifying detailed requirements. For example, an analyst might put together a use case on creating a new account, then add complexity by specifying requirements to add multiple people to the account, each needing separate credentials. Then, just in case one of the authorized people leaves, the analyst adds a requirement to be able to remove someone's access without losing the updates they've made. Suddenly, what began as a very simple requirement has become very complex.

Navigating scope creep ensures a truly valuable solution gets implemented. It's the business analyst's role to discover as many possibilities and options from the business as possible and partner with them to ensure the solution meets their needs, but it's also part of the role to ensure that the requirements stay within the scope.

Often, manual work-arounds are adequate for fringe exception cases. Not everything needs to be automated. Adding too many requirements and introducing too much complexity can derail the initiative's ROI or business case. Similarly, bloating the early features leaves little time and money to implement the remaining features or expectations.

Of course, it's not wrong to have more ideas than you can implement. Scope creep is a natural consequence of doing discovery, analysis, and understanding possibilities. To manage it successfully, regularly reevaluate your progress on the detailed requirements to ensure that every requirement truly generates business value, and that your team is focused on the most important requirements. Establish a habit of stepping back and looking at the big picture. Do the requirements fit into the project constraints? Will this project still deliver the ROI? Is it on track to deliver on the primary business objectives? Let the answers to these questions drive your next step, whether that be seeking approval for a change of scope, renegotiating some requirements, or creating a backlog of requirements for consideration during a follow-up phase or project. When complexity emerges inside a specific process or software feature, consider drafting two different versions of the deliverable—a basic version to prioritize early and a more advanced version to prioritize later if time and budget allow.[9] Another approach is to create one deliverable with all the proposed functionality and color-code or gray out the pieces that are being proposed for the future rather than included in the current initiative.

Preventing scope creep may require pushing back on business stakeholders who naturally want to generate as much value and as many capabilities as they can, sometimes to the point of becoming unreasonable or unrealistic. Providing as much information and as many options as possible helps prevent an us vs. them mentality. Acknowledge the constraints, such as an existing technology stack, available budget, and timeline, and share the options for generating the most possible value within those constraints. At the end of the day it's up to the business, in partnership with the implementation team, to decide whether a specific feature or requirement is in scope. Your role is to present the options and help them make the best decision possible.

One of the things I love about agile software development is the built-in mechanism for managing scope creep. Each new idea, requirement, configuration, or option becomes a new line item on the product backlog and the entire backlog gets rank prioritized sprint by sprint. You can't just bloat up a use case that's already listed as a line item on a project plan. Those new alternatives and exception flows become stories, and stories get prioritized.

Even if you aren't on an agile team, applying this sort of ruthless prioritization to your projects and requirements will help you optimize the value you create on your projects and leverage organizational resources efficiently.

---

[9] Many thanks to Meilir Page-Jones for this excellent suggestion!

►► Next Steps

This chapter covered the essentials of defining the detailed requirements, from discovering, to analyzing, to reviewing, validating, and finalizing every deliverable so it's ready for implementation. Here are some next steps to implement what you've learned:

- Identify the best strategies to discover information for each deliverable in your business analysis plan, ideally leveraging a combination of document analysis, interviews, and observation.
- Practice creating a requirements questionnaire to cultivate a focused and productive conversation.
- Analyze what you discover and draft a deliverable. Use structured analysis techniques to uncover gaps and generate more questions.
- Iterate through the review process until your team is ready to finalize the deliverable.
- Identify at least one idea to make your working meetings more productive, and ensure that every meeting you facilitate focuses on moving the project forward.
- Implement a regular review process to guard against scope creep.

Remember, your role is to ensure the business owns the solution and that the solution is technically feasible within the constraints of the change effort. This requires a lot of negotiation, and iterative work on a deliverable is to be expected.

Keep working this process through one deliverable after another. The next two chapters provide additional techniques for detailed requirements on software initiatives.

6

Analyzing the Software Requirements

This chapter explores techniques for creating clarity about the software requirements. It covers ideas for integrating use cases, wireframes, user stories, and product backlogs efficiently, and for deciding on the best approach to analyze the software requirements for your project and team.

The essence of this skill set is getting business and technology stakeholders on the same page about what the software needs to do to solve a business problem, whether it's being custom-coded or, more likely, licensed, implemented, and configured. Without this clarity, software teams invest significant resources building or customizing software that does not deliver business value. Often called "missed requirements" or a "requirements defect," this wastes massive amounts of resources, contributes to employee discontent, and degrades trust within and among the business and technology teams.

While there are many valid approaches to analyzing software requirements, I believe use cases and wireframes are foundational analysis techniques. Combining the written software requirements in a use case with a visual model like a wireframe is incredibly powerful, creating breakthroughs in clarity and alignment at a detailed, functional level. I've found that business analysts who learn how to think in use cases can explain what the software needs to do using language that business users can understand. They also tend to miss fewer requirements. Meanwhile, your stakeholders see the full potential of the solution and provide clarifying feedback in more efficient ways.

Product backlogs and user stories are also important. Many agile teams expect to receive information in the user story format. Packaging requirements in a structured, rank-prioritized way is necessary when working with agile software development teams, and encourages meaningful prioritization by the business.

Consider these questions when choosing how to analyze software requirements:

- What do my developers need from me to be successful?
- What's the most efficient way for me to communicate this information?
- What techniques can I use to ensure my analysis is complete and I ask all the questions I need to ask?
- What techniques will help me get the best possible input from my business stakeholders?
- How can I protect myself and my team from unnecessary change and scope creep?

These questions will help you stay focused on value-driven outcomes while ensuring the deliverables you create service the diverse needs of your team.

The Power of Use Case Thinking

"Use case thinking" sounds good, but what does it mean to think in use cases?

Whenever I call a customer support line, I'm aware that I'm inter-acting with a software system. There are prompts and how I respond to those prompts (whether via voice or keypad clicks) is going to elicit a specific system response. I often find myself analyzing the hierarchy of options, why one thing leads to another, and what information is collected when.

I inevitably become frustrated when the system asks for my account number multiple times, when I have to answer multiple prompts when one could get me to the right information or representative, or when the system shares my account balance when I didn't request it. But then I wonder, do people actually call to get their balance? Is there a reason that this data needs to be collected multiple times? Who is the hierarchy of prompts set up to weed out?

As you internalize the structure of the use case, it becomes a mental model that helps you quickly see gaps and ask better questions:

- What must be true before the user can take that action?
- Who is responsible for that step?
- What *exactly* are you expecting the system to do when you click that button?
- How do we know this action is successful?
- Does the system need to save any data?
- What must be done with the data?
- What happens if _____?

Use case thinking also breaks down barriers of communication between business and technology stakeholders, and helps everyone collaborate. In learning to write a use case, business analysts with a business background start to understand the solution from a technical perspective, and those from a technical background start to understand the solution from a business perspective.

Use case thinking is *not* technical design. You do not have to know how to code to write use cases. In fact, those with a technical background must learn how to craft use cases in clear language that a business user can understand, and resist any temptation to include pseudocode or technical details.

Similarly, while the use case may include steps from a business process, a use case is *not* a business process. It only includes business process steps in which a user specifically interacts with the software solution under design. Further, a use case must be specific and detailed about what the software needs to do, which often is not described in a business process document.

You learn to think in use cases by writing them.

Analyzing Software Requirements in a Use Case

A use case is a text description of how a human user interacts with a software system (a solution) to achieve a specific goal or outcome that's valuable to them. A complete use case will describe all the possible outcomes a solution needs to handle during a user's attempt to accomplish a particular goal.

Ivar Jacobson created the use case technique in the 1990s, and describes it as "all the ways of using a system to achieve a particular goal for a particular user."[10] In the context of a use case, a user goal is something that the software system can support and accomplish. User goals should relate back to the business objectives, but a business objective itself would be too big for a user goal in a use case.

For example, imagine a business objective to reduce time spent securing new customers by 10 hours. After evaluating the business process, the business analyst uncovers time-intensive activities required to follow up with potential leads. The team decides to delegate some activities to a new role in sales support and automate others with system-generated follow-ups. A meaningful use case goal would be to "schedule automated follow-up messages so we can keep in touch with our highest-value leads."

[10] Ivar Jacobson International, "Use Cases – The Ultimate Guide," January 11, 2024, https://www.ivarjacobson.com/publications/articles/use-cases-ultimate-guide.

Avoid specifying goals that go beyond the scope of the use case. For example, a goal to "close more sales" would be too big for a use case, although the goal for scheduling automated follow-up messages would certainly support this objective.

But neither should goals be too technically focused. They need to be meaningful to a *human* user. A goal such as "trigger API in email marketing system" is not meaningful to the user, while "send follow-up message" (which may be accomplished by triggering the API in the email marketing system) is.

When considering goals for use cases, evaluate whether a software system could be expected to help the user to achieve the goal directly and whether someone such as a software tester could verify that this goal was accomplished.

Use Case Example: Book Ride

Download an annotated use case template in the Business Analyst Success Pack.

Brief Description
The purpose of this use case is to enable a customer to book a ride using a ride-sharing service. This use case starts when the customer selects "book a ride" and ends when the ride is confirmed.

Actors
- Customer
- Driver

Preconditions
- Customer is logged into the ride-sharing system.
- Customer has location tracking active on their device.
- Customer has valid payment information stored in their account profile.

Basic Flow

1. The Customer selects "book a ride."
2. The Ride Booking System requests the Customer's target location.
3. The Customer provides their target location.
4. The Ride Booking System searches available Drivers near the Customer's current location and finds up to three ride options.
5. The Ride Booking System displays the location, price, estimated arrival time, and fuel efficiency for each ride option.
6. The Customer selects one ride option.
7. The Ride Booking System presents the terms of service.
8. The Customer agrees to the terms of service.
9. The Customer confirms the booking.
10. The Driver confirms the booking.
11. The Ride Booking System saves confirmation details.
12. The Ride Booking System presents the confirmation to the Customer and Driver.

Alternate Flows

6a—Customer's selected ride option is not available.
- The Ride Booking System determines that the ride option is no longer available.
- The Ride Booking System presents a message to the Customer.
- Continue with Step 4.

10a—Driver declines booking.
- The Ride Booking System presents a message to the Customer.
- Continue with Step 4.

Exception Flows

4a—No ride options available
- The Ride Booking System presents an error message to the Customer.
- Use Case ends.

6b—Customer does not select ride option.
- After 60 seconds, the Ride Booking System presents a warning message.
- After 120 seconds, the Ride Booking System clears the ride options.
- Use Case ends.

Post Conditions
- Confirmation details are saved.

Key Use Case Concepts

Let's look at each section of the use case.

- **Use Case Name** – Usually written in *verb noun* form, the name clarifies the specific user goal that the use case will accomplish.
- **Brief Description** – Summarize the functionality the use case describes, and include a "starts when / ends when" statement that creates a clear boundary around the use case by describing the scope of the process from a user's perspective.
- **Actors** – An actor is a specific type of user, or a role with a collection of abilities or permissions, within the context of the system. Actor names do not need to align to the job titles in the organization.
- **Preconditions** – Preconditions describe what the solution can assume to be true when the use case begins. The

system must be able to validate the preconditions, so they can't be an idea in the user's head or a business process step that happens outside the system (such as receiving an email).

- **Basic Flow** – The basic flow describes a set of back-and-forth user steps and system responses that happen in sequence and enable the user to accomplish the goal of the use case, assuming nothing out of the ordinary occurs and nothing goes wrong. Write steps in active, not passive voice, to avoid introducing ambiguity. (For example, "Customer selects ride" or "System searches for options" rather than "Ride is selected" or "Options are found.")
- **Alternate Flows** – Alternate flows are variations from the basic flow that still result in the user goal being completed, like a branch of the main flow. Take care to identify the specific step where the alternate flow begins, describe step-by-step what happens during the alternate flow, and identify where the main flow picks back up again. Asking, "what else can happen?" makes for a great discovery question when reviewing a use case.
- **Exception Flows** – Exception flows are variations that result in the user *not* achieving the goal of the use case. They are written exactly like alternate flows, but typically start with the system identifying an error condition and end with "Use Case ends." Some practitioners combine alternate flows and exception flows, and structurally they are the same. I believe keeping them separate leads to better analysis and more questions.
- **Post Conditions** – Post conditions describe the state of the system once the use case is complete, and should apply for all scenarios through the basic flow and alternate flows. A post condition must happen as a result of a step in the

basic or alternate flow. Because exception flows can end
the use case prematurely, not all post conditions will be
fulfilled when an exception is triggered.

An important nuance is to ensure that each step focuses on the
point of interaction between the user and the solution. This weeds
out extraneous information such as business process details or bits
of technical design.

Be sure to keep the system response in mind when writing use
cases. Business analysts from a business background often struggle
with getting to the right level of detail about what the software is
actually supposed to do, creating ambiguity and missed requirements.
They tend to get into a lot of detail about the user steps and gloss over
system steps. Always ask, What does the software system need to do
in response to this user action? Include that action as a system step in
the use case.

In contrast, business analysts with a technical background tend
do the reverse and leave out user steps when writing a user case.
They also often communicate requirements using tech speak that
business users cannot understand and provide meaningful feedback
on. Always ask, What does the user need to do to prompt this system
step? Or, How will the system know to do this, and what information
will it need? Include those actions as user steps in the use case.

The structure of the use case encourages us to tread this user–
system line, and that's what makes the use case syntax so powerful
as an analysis and elicitation technique. This is what strong analytical and solution-focused thinking about the software requirements
looks like.

Most people learn to write use cases one at a time, but on a
project you will rarely write a single use case. Often, you will write
a collection of use cases to completely cover the initiative scope,
and these use cases should all be identified in the business analysis

plan. The use case example above is only one of the cases needed for a ride-sharing application. A real-world project would have several more:

- Turn On Driver Availability
- Provide Payment Information
- Update Ride
- Schedule Ride
- Set Up Rider Profile
- Bill for Ride
- Pay Driver
- Set Up Driver Profile

It's also not uncommon for one use case to lead to another, particularly as you identify preconditions and create detailed flows. If a use case gets too complex, narrowing the goal of the use case and analyzing one part of the system at a time can reduce complexity.

Use Cases for COTS Projects

As previously discussed, it's increasingly uncommon for teams to build new custom software from scratch. More often, the organization buys or licenses access to COTS systems that can be configured and sometimes customized to meet specific needs and requirements.

Business analysts on these projects often sidestep a lot of software requirements analysis, since the software is already built. And while it's true that functional and software requirements effort should be a lighter lift on a COTS initiative, that doesn't mean it's nonexistent. Use cases can add a lot of value by exploring complex areas of functionality *before* anyone invests time and energy in making configurations.

An example is Jami Moore's work on a large-scale Salesforce upgrade at a medical device company. One of the decisions her team struggled with was the business consumer model. They wanted to explore how to use Salesforce's person account as part of their implementation. Jami put together her first-ever use case, and it helped the business partners understand how the team could build out the module and everything that would have to happen from the end user perspective. Her business sponsor was enthusiastic: "I've never ever seen it done this way and this is fantastic." She then built a presentation for her architect team and higher-level executives to help them get up to speed on the module and why it was the right configuration for their organization.

Use cases are a fantastic tool to get specific about the software functionality while honoring the big picture, and they can support your efforts to gain buy-in from business and technology stakeholders on a solution approach.

Still, there are use cases that it would make no sense to write on a COTS project. For example, I love presenting a Login use case when teaching because it is simple and commonly understood. But unless the organization has enhanced cyber security requirements, it would be unusual to change the login functionality for a COTS system, and writing a use case for Login would only be asking for scope creep. For a COTS project, focus on the areas of functionality where you are exploring configuration options and specifying customizations. Keep discussion of how to use existing functionality to achieve business goals in the business process models, rather than the use cases.

As powerful and understandable as use cases are, they are still text-based models. Leveraging visuals such as wireframes to supplement your use case writing and thinking tends to improve stakeholder engagement.

Enhance Your Productivity with Generative AI

- Request a use case draft, using the template in the
  Business Analyst Success Pack to train AI to create the
  style of use case described in this chapter.
- Upload a draft use case and ask for alternate and
  exception flows.
- Build a use case list from a scope statement or other
  documentation.
- Review and critique a use case for language, flow,
  and best practices.
- Update a use case based on a meeting discussion.

Using Wireframes to Visualize Requirements

Text-based models tell stakeholders how the system will function; a wireframe shows them what the system will look like. Wireframes are the perfect accompaniment to use cases because most of stakeholders will understand pictures more quickly than text.

On one project with particularly challenging stakeholders, I had done everything I could think of to encourage them to stay focused on the requirements in the use case. I prepared agendas. I visually shared the use case. I printed the use case and provided physical copies in meetings. I referred to the use case again and again to refocus the discussion. It seemed that no matter what I did, the conversation would veer to ideas well beyond the scope of the use case.

Finally, in a burst of inspiration, I shared a wireframe on the screen. Almost immediately, I captured their attention. Our discussion actually stayed on track. From that point on, I prepared use cases annotated with all my questions and used the wireframe to talk through all the business rules, user–system behavior, and analysis questions. We got so much done so quickly! In this case we were meeting in person, but the same approach would work for a remote meeting as well.

Business analysts sometimes complain about the time required to create a wireframe, but if you spent more than a half hour you are overcomplicating it or using the wrong tool. With a bit of practice, you'll be able to create a decent wireframe in 10 minutes or less. Plus, any time you invest in creating an effective wireframe should save you loads of time in meetings and make the entire requirements process more efficient.

Key Wireframe Concepts

A *wireframe,* also called a mock-up, is an abstract representation of a user interface. Close cousins to wireframes include prototypes, renderings, and simulations, which tend to be higher-fidelity functional models rather than static, informal screens.

A *user interface* is the means by which a user (most often a human user) interacts with a system (most often a piece of software). A user interface is a collection of interconnected screens that present information to a user, provide options for the user to take specific actions, and connect to the underlying systems that process information and respond to user actions. Websites, mobile phone applications, and installed software systems all have user interfaces.

To use wireframes efficiently, be sure to choose the right level of fidelity:

- **Low Fidelity** focuses on the general layout of one possible arrangement of elements on the screen, often using grayscale so colors and fonts are deliberately unspecified.
- **Medium Fidelity** puts the right information in the right places, and may be accurate about the text displayed on the page and on various elements of the page.

- **High Fidelity** represents exactly how the user interface
  should look and feel. It includes specific colors, fonts,
  spacing, and sometimes graphics that can be built into
  the implemented web page or application.

In requirements discovery and analysis activities, stick with
low- or medium-fidelity models. You want to be able to easily make
changes, rearrange entire screens, and move information from one
screen to another without wasting hours of work. What's more,
when you make things too pretty too early, your stakeholders tend
to focus on colors and button placement instead of functionality.
Keeping your wireframes informal helps elicit feedback on the actual functional requirements and workflow of the user interface and
system. As the requirements are validated, it can make sense to create a higher-fidelity model, although that's often the responsibility
of a front-end developer or user experience designer.

Here's what a medium-fidelity wireframe might look like. This
wireframe was created using Balsamiq, which creates electronic
versions of what look like hand-drawn wireframes—a great way to
keep things simple and informal.

Figure 10. A medium-fidelity wireframe for a job search website

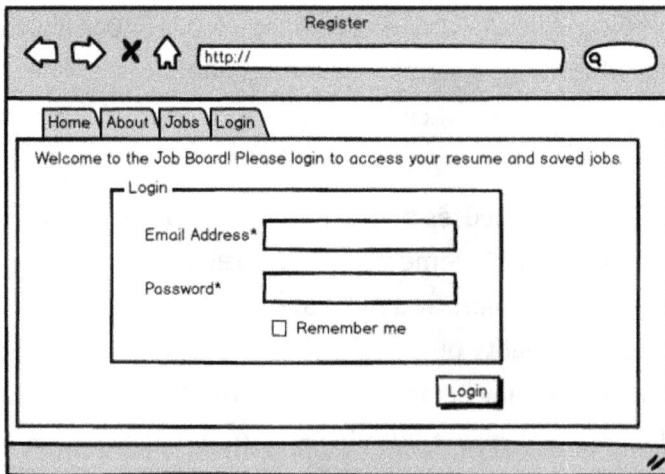

This model contains three main elements:

- A screen or page or other collection of content a user can see at one time on their device. Each wireframe represents a single screen or page.
- Navigation menus, often along the top or side of the screen, that provide access to functions and tend to be consistent across screens.
- On-page elements that would be displayed on the screen, which can include text, fields to capture data, and buttons to execute functions.

Figure 11. Common page elements used in wireframes

Element	Example	When to Use
Text Box		When a user can use a field to enter a data point, such as a name or email address.
Text Area		When a user can use a field to enter a lot of data, such as the text of an email.
Pick List or Drop Down	Selection 1 ▼ Selection 2 Selection 3	When a user can scroll through a list to choose a single item.
Check Box(es)	☐ not selected ☑ selected	When a user can check a single box to select an option or multiple boxes to enable multiple selections.
Radio Button	◉ option 1 (selected) ○ option 2	When a user can make a single selection from a list displayed completely on the screen.
Date Chooser	/ / ▦	To restrict user entry when the field requires a date.
Button	Button	For a primary user action on a page, often used to submit the information provided in the form.
Text Link	Here is a text link	For a secondary user action on a page, such as a link to an FAQ or another page on the site.

Business Analysis in User Interface Modeling

The role of a business analyst in user interface modeling can vary widely. I have created simple, low-fidelity mock-ups, created medium-fidelity wireframes, and even used elements provided by a graphic designer to model high-fidelity renderings, albeit with a cut-and-paste look.

I'm not a graphic designer by trade so I do not have the skills required to create images or choose colors and fonts, yet I have successfully helped many teams get crystal clear on their visual requirements. For the record, I am also not a software developer or a web designer; everything I have done has been with user-friendly drag-and-drop tools that are accessible for anyone comfortable using software.

To figure out your role in the user interface modeling process, start by evaluating the expertise available on your team. Look for titles and job functions such as user interface designer, information architect, product manager, usability professional, or user interface developer (or another member of the software development team who tends to do design work).

More often than not, the team will include someone who is an expert in graphic design or user interface design. You need to figure out how best to collaborate with them, treating them as a stake-holder in the functional requirements process and when creating user interface models. There are several ways this can play out:

- **Collaboration with a user interface designer.** The business analyst develops low-fidelity wireframes and the designer owns the higher-fidelity renderings, or even web-ready code, for a representative set of screens.
- **Creating wireframes for an existing application (including COTS).** When the system already exists, the business

analyst can often mock up changes by manipulating a combination of screenshots and wireframing elements to show how new or updated screens should look.

- **Analyzing pre-existing high-fidelity models.** When a user interface designer starts work before the functional requirements are validated, the business analyst can use the models as part of discovery, provide feedback on these models to get them aligned to the finalized functional requirements, or mock up changes as you would for an existing application.

Be really, really careful not to step on toes and wander into someone else's area of expertise during this process. If your team has qualified designers, let them shine. Your goal in wireframing is not to take over their work; it's to model the system to the lowest level of detail needed to get alignment on the detailed requirements. Learn about the expertise on your team first, and build relationships with anyone doing user interface-related work. But don't overlook opportunities to create quick-and-dirty visual models that will facilitate better discussions.

Now that you have a foundational understanding of use cases and wireframes, let's consider the specific ways business analysts contribute to agile software development teams. The agile environment can shift expectations in terms of the deliverables business analysts create and methods of discovering, validating, and finalizing software requirements.

✔ Succeeding in Agile: Product Backlogs and User Stories

Agile teams focus a lot of attention on product backlogs and user stories. Because of that, a lot of professionals assume that when working with an agile software development team, all you need are user stories, and that's simply not the case.

I fell into this trap myself on my first agile team. Wanting to be a team player, and being new to agile, I jumped in with reckless abandon. Instead of drafting a use case list as part of my business analysis plan and working through the use cases with corresponding wireframes, I drafted a product backlog and started working through the user stories.

This worked well at first, but after four or five sprints we had a lot of leftover product backlog items that were needed to round out incomplete features. It was difficult for the business to see the big picture and meaningfully prioritize the remaining items. It was difficult for me to analytically think through how all the pieces fit together and uncover requirements gaps. So I stepped back and created a high-level workflow diagram to capture the scope of the product and link it to the product backlog, highlighting what had been implemented and what was still outstanding.

Few people who teach user stories today teach them as a stand-alone technique. Usually, user stories are accompanied by other analytical tools, particularly wireframes and data models. It's also common to use a variety of techniques to look at the big picture in agile environments, such as story maps, epics, and release plans.

I like to think of the product backlog and user stories as my primary touchpoint with the software development team so they have the information they need to implement the solution. But they are not enough by themselves. That's one reason this book contains a tool-box full of different techniques, as well as guidance on when to use what.

Today I teach use cases and wireframes first, as a way to look at the big-picture flow of a feature, and then help participants break apart their use cases into a product backlog and user stories, if that's the way they need to communicate requirements to their software development team. Some will continue that practice in their regular work, others will start with a product backlog and user stories, and back into use cases when a user story is complex and requires more comprehensive analysis. Use case thinking is valuable even when writing user stories.

Not all agile teams leverage use cases. You can also generate a product backlog by decomposing an epic, a story map, a business processes, or any other bigger-picture view of the scope and business objectives for the next phase of the initiative. This section will discuss ways you can leverage use cases, wireframes, business process models, or any other techniques you are using to analyze the big picture and organize it into a product backlog and user stories so you can communicate effectively with an agile software development team. Although this is not a book on agile as a methodology or software development practice, most business analysts today will interface with agile teams and need to understand what's expected. We'll begin by looking at the end result—the user story.

Understanding User Stories

The cornerstone of each product backlog item, the user story, is a single statement in the following syntax:

"As a **[user]**, I can **[do something]** so that **[perceived benefit]**."

Let's look at each part of the syntax separately:

- **As a [User]** – The story starts with "As a [user]," where [user] is the name of a user or actor from the use case. In the example of Book Ride, the users are the Customer and the Driver, or the actors of the use case.
- **I can [do something]** – This describes what the user can actually do, or the functional requirement to be met by the software system.

- **So that [perceived benefit]** – This explains the why behind the functional requirement. Other terms for this would be the business benefit, justification, rationale, or anticipated ROI. This is a powerful aspect of the user story syntax, and it's what made me fall just a little bit in love with agile practices and possibilities.

Figure 12. Example user stories for the Book Ride use case

As a [user]	I can [do something]	So that [perceived benefit]
Customer	Specify my target location	I can find rides that will get me where I want to go.
Customer	View available ride options	I can find the ride that best suits my preferences.
Customer	Select a ride option	I can choose the ride that best suits my preferences.
Customer	Confirm a booking	I lock in my preferred ride option.
Driver	Confirm a booking	I can receive income from providing a ride.

Figure 12 shows a list of possible user stories for the Book Ride use case. A list like this is a *product backlog*. As in this example, the basic flow of a use case tends to split into several user stories. There could also be a user story for each alternate and exception flow.

Even though each user story delivers business value, the stories themselves are development focused. They become units of work for an agile team. A team works on several user stories in a sprint—a duration of work typically lasting two to four weeks—and delivers immediate value to the business.

To build a product backlog, start by drafting a list of stories and then collaborate with the development team to look for opportunities to combine simpler stories or split up complex ones. In this case, the "View available ride options" seems big; it involves all the logic needed to search for available rides and present them in a user-friendly way. And "Select a ride option" seems like it could be combined with "Confirm a booking."

Agile teams often agree to a maximum estimated development effort before a user story must be broken apart and reprioritized. For example, a team might decide that all user stories should be implementable within three business days. Any user stories larger than this would be broken apart. This means that every user story gets estimated.

Many teams use story points to estimate their backlog items. Others assign hours. Then, as the development team goes into sprint planning, they have an allocated number of points or hours that they can do. These estimates can also help you plan your business analysis work, so you can stay just far enough ahead of the development team.

Although user stories are development focused, that does not mean they should be about isolated pieces of code or aspects of the design, like "implement stored procedure" or "set up a web form." Ideally, the user story will represent a thread of work that is observable and valuable to the user, and enables them to realize the "so that" value in the user story. The benefit might be incremental, and the team may need to implement several user stories to meet a business objective. Yet each discrete user story, once implemented, should deliver a requirement that has at least some independent value to the business. As the user stories stack up, the team meets that overall business objective.

Collaborating with Agile Teams

Because the user stories literally represent where business meets software, the business analyst can be at the heart of the collaborative effort of developing and maintaining the product backlog. It's a good practice to have a regular meeting with developers where you discuss and estimate new backlog items, get their feedback on solution options and considerations, and work together to ensure the product backlog makes sense from a technical implementation perspective. Similarly, you want to meet regularly with business stakeholders to refine user stories, prioritize the backlog, and learn about new requests.

The team workflow could look like this:

1. The business analyst identifies potential product backlog items. (These may be derived from the use cases, scope documents, business process models, story maps, epics, or other requirements documents.)
2. The business analyst and developers review the product backlog, breaking apart or combining user stories as appropriate.
3. The business analyst works with the business stakeholders to rank prioritize the product backlog, or at least the first batch of items in the backlog. (Combining this with backlog review is a great option and can eliminate a lot of back-and-forth time, but can be more challenging to manage.)
4. The developers estimate the work involved with each user story, while the business analyst provides clarifications related to scope or intent.
5. The business analyst confirms the backlog ranking with the business, given the estimates the developers provided.
6. The business analyst provides supporting details for the user story, to enable implementation.

7. The team selects one or more backlog items for a sprint during a sprint planning session, choosing the next set of user stories by looking at the highest-priority items and selecting from that list until the allocated points or hours are used up. The business analyst provides information around business impacts and priorities to help guide the selection.

8. The business analyst supports the team during the sprint by answering questions and providing clarifying information as they implement the story.

It's best practice for the business analyst to be working a sprint or two ahead of development, so that they go into a planning session with a well-defined set of user stories that are ready for implementation.

Another piece of ongoing work is revising the product backlog. As user stories get evaluated, pieces may fall out or become too time-intensive. The business analyst adds these pieces of functionality to the product backlog as new user stories. As product backlog items surface for approaching sprints, further estimates and ranking may be needed to support an effective sprint planning meeting.

Agile business analysts are continually managing and revising the product backlog, capturing estimates from development, working with the business to rank prioritize backlog items, and analyzing each story to ensure it's ready for development to start implementing—or collaborating with and supporting the product owner in all of the above. As always, where there are overlapping and parallel roles, take time to work through a shared understanding of responsibilities.

While developing the product backlog and collaborating with the implementation team to make it workable, it often makes sense to capture additional information about each product backlog item.

The product backlog can be maintained in a spreadsheet or an agile planning tool, with many other criteria specified about each item:

- ID
- status
- date identified
- target sprint
- submitter
- systems impacted
- actors/users impacted
- business stakeholders
- technical stakeholders
- related use case (or epic, story map, or business process)
- estimate
- rank
- related user stories

These criteria help the team organize and sift through a long list of user stories and product backlog items.

Developing Acceptance Criteria

As you refine the backlog, add more details to the user stories so they include the information necessary for implementation. On some teams, these details come out through active conversations. As important as conversations and collaboration are, a written record helps everyone be more effective and efficient. Most often, acceptance criteria are used to clarify expectations and detail requirements.

Acceptance criteria are the conditions a software product must satisfy to be accepted by a user, customer, or other stakeholder—a set of statements that can clearly be confirmed through testing, with a result of pass or fail.

Let's look at an example using the following product backlog item.

"As a Customer, I can specify my target location so that I can find rides that will get me where I want to go."

The acceptance criteria for this product backlog item might read as follows:

- When a Customer selects "book a ride," the Ride Booking System presents the ride booking form.
- If the system is not able to identify the Customer's current location, the Ride Booking System presents an error message and does not allow the Customer to continue booking until location tracking is turned on.
- When a Customer provides a target location in the form of an address, the Ride Booking System uses that address as the target location.
- When a Customer provides a target location in the form of a geodata point, the Ride Booking System first looks for nearby addresses and landmarks to confirm the Customer's precise target location.
- When the customer does not provide a target location within 3 minutes, the Ride Booking System resets and removes the ride booking form from the display.

If you are finding it challenging to come up with specific acceptance criteria, experiment with writing a use case for the functionality around your user story. Often this will help you see the bigger picture so you can drill into the specific details needed for each user story.

It's also common to provide additional supporting documentation to supplement the acceptance criteria in a user story:

- wireframes that show any screens related to the user story
- use cases or business process models that have the big-picture context for the specific requirements in the user story

- data models, such as a data dictionary, that have the details for specific data elements being collected or updated

When in doubt, ask your developers what they most need. Unlike use cases, which are often maintained long term as part of comprehensive system documentation, user stories are throwaway documents. Make sure they serve their sole purpose, which is communication with the development team, in the best possible way.

Enhance Your Productivity with Generative AI

- Request a wireframe to visualize a use case.
- Break apart a use case into a product backlog and user stories.
- Generate acceptance tests.
- Group and sort through product backlog items by business priorities.

▶▶ Next Steps

This chapter explored three techniques—use cases, wireframes, and user stories—that work alone or together to support the discovery, analysis, and validation of software requirements. This set of techniques support the analysis and validation of the detailed requirements work in step 5, whether you find yourself on a traditional, agile, or hybrid team.

Here are some next steps to implement what you've learned:
- Practice writing a use case, taking care to identify both user and system steps in clear, active business language. What clarity emerges? How can you leverage use case writing or thinking in your initiatives going forward?

- Explore roles and capabilities on your team related to user interface development. Practice creating a few low- or medium-fidelity wireframes as part of the discovery and review process.
- Try breaking apart a use case into a product backlog of user stories.
- Collaborate with your development team to confirm the types of details to include in your user stories (or any other type of software requirements documentation) to ensure they can effectively implement the solution.

As you consider your options, remember that both use cases and user stories have pros and cons.

Compared to use cases, a user story approach:

- helps control scope creep,
- integrates well with agile software development teams and improves planning, and
- empowers the business to rank prioritize requirements.

Compared to user stories, a use case approach:

- provides a bigger-picture perspective that puts the software requirements in context of user goals and activities,
- provides a structure that encourages good analytical thinking and raises valid requirements questions, and
- provides a structure for capturing current-state system documentation that can be kept up-to-date over the course of subsequent projects.

The world is full of false either-or choices, and the use case versus user story debate encourages this sort of either-or thinking.

Both-and is a valid choice, and leverages the best of both use cases and user stories, along with wireframes, to ensure the most value-driven combination of analytical thinking and clear communication when it comes to software requirements.

7

Modeling the Business Domain and Analyzing Data Requirements

When it comes to discovering, analyzing, and modeling requirements, our language matters. Just ask stakeholders from three different departments to define "customer." Chances are, they'll have three or more different interpretations of how to use this term, unless they've never even thought to clarify what "customer" means because it seems so obvious.

Except it's not. And if you use the term "customer" in your business process and software requirements documentation without defining it, your so-called clear requirements will not be clear at all.

Chapter 1 discussed how to start building a glossary to capture key terms, definitions, and acronyms to help you sort through the overwhelming deluge of information that tends to come your way early in an initiative. This chapter explores a set of techniques that will help you structure that understanding of the business language in a meaningful, logical way.

As we build software applications or information systems, we basically embed our terminology into our business solutions. Yet many organizations have mountains of information they don't understand. For example, one of my clients had invested several months implementing an expensive business intelligence system but still could not generate meaningful reports to support data-driven decision-making.

My role was to work through the end-to-end business process, software, and data requirements so they could achieve the intended return on their huge investment. Interestingly, the data model updates were the least significant aspect of the project. Most changes involved making sure their expensive business intelligence system held meaningful information by realigning the business processes and the functional flow of the software to capture information at the right time and in the right way. Occasionally, we also updated a software screen to capture a new piece of information and made a relatively minor update to pass that data element to the business intelligence system.

The most challenging part of many change efforts is when data gets migrated from one system to another, particularly when shifting to a new COTS application or when there is an ongoing need to integrate data between systems. Despite surface-level parallels, it's incredibly common to face massive issues with missing fields, different data types, truncated information, or conflicting business rules that cause significant delays and last-minute rework.

These days, it's less likely that a business analyst will be responsible for detailed data modeling. Data-intensive projects require professionals with specialized skill sets such as data analysis, data warehousing, and business intelligence applications. Still, be sure to understand what's happening with the data so you can communicate effectively with database architects and designers to ensure that business concerns are addressed and business outcomes are realized. The best way to prepare for this kind of work is to ensure that you understand the business domain and have some basic data or information-modeling skills.

We've already discussed two parts of this: the chapter 1 discussion of glossaries, and the chapter 3 coverage of system context diagrams, which show how data flows from one system to another. This chapter will discuss three foundational domain modeling techniques: business domain diagrams, data dictionaries, and data maps. These techniques will set you up to be a more active and prepared contributor on data-focused projects, as well as on system integration and migration projects.

Analyzing Business Concepts in a Domain Model

The first business domain model I ever created was for my second business analyst role, working in a new organization with relatively unfamiliar systems and some unfamiliar domain language. We were building a new product to help our customers research scientific information, and one of our goals was to enable them to seamlessly order reproductions of articles. We had a legacy system that contained customer and article information, and we were a few months into developing the new system but hadn't explored how it would connect to the legacy system. To complicate matters, there were two technical teams—an internal team for the legacy system and a third-party consulting organization that was responsible for building the new product—and they weren't talking to each other.

I began to sense that this lack of communication, and perhaps more importantly, database architecture, was a significant risk, but was overshadowed by schedule pressures to build one piece of front-facing functionality after another. No one had considered how these two systems would be integrated and how the data would support the functional requirements.

The technical lead suggested I create a domain model to sort out the integration issue. I like a challenge, so I picked up a book on Unified Modeling Language (UML) and started working my way through the analysis of a class diagram. I soon realized we had two different definitions of "customer" to reconcile, and that even the connections between article information were not as clear as I originally assumed.

After several collaborative (albeit sticky) sessions, we had ironed out how to get the two systems to talk to one another and I had a domain model I could use as a touchstone when analyzing functional requirements related to the integration, such as creating a new customer account, setting up customer access to the new system, and ordering an article. It turned out that I needed to understand this level of detail to be effective when specifying my more detailed functional requirements and helping business stakeholders understand how their business processes would change. Many stakeholders quickly understood the model.

I've created business domain models several other times in my career, turning to this technique whenever we needed to get a handle on how the data is or should be organized. These models are particularly useful for system integration and migration efforts. A business domain model will often help you and your team get unstuck when you have jumped into technical details too fast or are having trouble getting clear on requirements language. What's more, a good business domain model will be a huge gift to a database architect, providing a business-focused starting point for developing a more technical and complex physical database model.

The primary point of a business domain model is to show how business concepts relate to one another logically. There are three basic elements of the structure: concepts, relationships, and attributes. Figure 13 shows a very simple sample business domain model.

Figure 13. A business domain model for instructional software

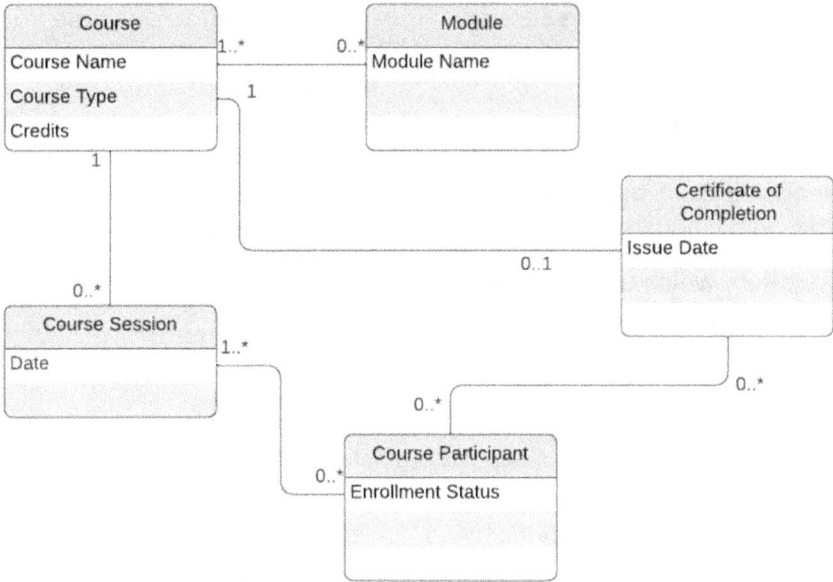

Let's look at each element of this model:

- **Concepts** – First, there are the boxes. Each box represents a business concept in business terms. You can often pull these from your glossary. Think of them as containers of information, or as records. Each box is named with a business concept, for example, "Course" and "Course Session."

- **Attributes** – Next, there are the additional line items within each box. These represent the fields, or attributes, associated with the concept. For example, the concept "Course" would have specific attributes for the Course Name, Course Type, and Credits.

- **Relationships** – Finally there are the lines connecting the boxes, which represent the relationships between concepts. The text at the end of each line represents the number of possible relationships. For example, the Course concept can have any number of Course Sessions or none at all (0..*), but each Course Session, if it exists, is related to only one Course (1).

UML notation allows four different multiplicities that can be specified on a business domain model as part of a class diagram (see figure 14). An alternative to UML multiplicities is crow's foot notation, which uses graphics to represent the same four variations. I have a strong preference for the multiplicity notation, because I find it more intuitive.

Figure 14. Valid multiplicities and cardinalities (concept relationships) in UML

Multiplicity	Cardinality	Description
1	‖	One and only one
1...*	⫡	Any number (one to many)
0...1	⊸	Zero to one
0...*	⤙	Any number (zero to many)

Discovering the relationships between concepts is where the real analytical work happens. To find relationships, pick any two concepts you've defined and ask whether and how they relate. Another way to ask this question is: Could either concept exist without the other? When two concepts are related in a way that is important to the business, evaluate how the concepts exist numerically in relation to one another.

This is a great task to complete in collaboration with business and technical stakeholders. Ask them to describe the relationship between two terms. As the team agrees on a relationship, update the relationship line to capture the discussion. Move on to another two concepts until all the possibilities are exhausted. When meeting in person, I like to hand out my printed draft to use as a starting point and then draw the domain model on the white board so we have a lot of creative freedom to explore concepts and relationships. In a virtual setting, you could send your draft in advance and present a blank virtual white board, moving in pieces of your draft as you discuss them.

Don't be surprised if this requires some iteration. I revised the simple domain model in figure 13 several times, and made several updates to the corresponding glossary. Significantly, I realized that the terms I had listed for Course, Membership, and Workshop were all variations on a Course, so instead of creating separate concepts for each, I created one Course concept and added a Type attribute to capture that information.

It's natural to revise definitions and uncover new relationships as you begin to model the terms in your glossary. This is the power of looking at your information model from both a visual and a text-based perspective. Each structure prompts new understanding.

Practicing this technique will improve your collaboration with the technical team. Several participants have told me that after learning this skill they can speak the same language as their tech leads or database administrators, provide critical business input on data models, and ask intelligent questions in technical meetings.

One caveat: The business domain model looks like a database design, so be sure to emphasize that it's a conceptual model focusing on the business concepts, and not a database design. When reviewing these models with technical stakeholders I ask them to set aside their detailed knowledge of the actual database design for the purposes of the discussion, and focus on understanding the business domain conceptually while we talk through the model. This can be hard for them to do, but the aha moments that percolate as a result are valuable.

If your team struggles with this model, you can make it less rigorous by swapping out boxes for circles, leaving out the attributes, and using words to describe the multiplicity, as shown in figure 15.

Figure 15. A simplified business domain model

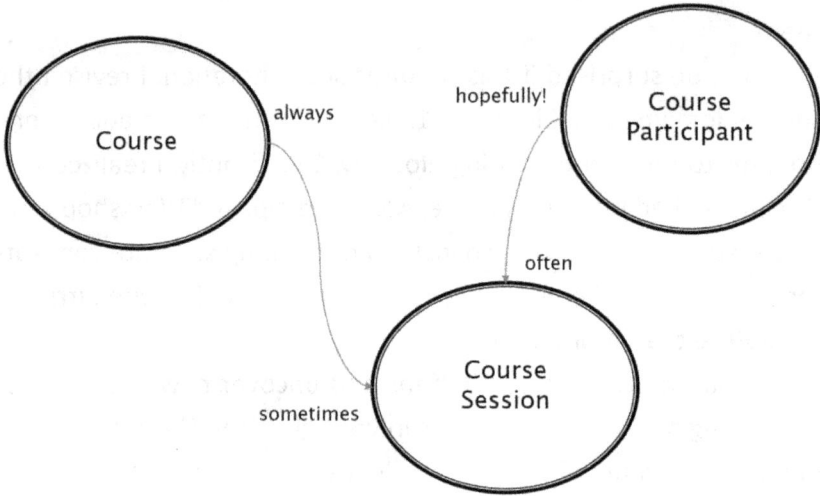

As powerful as business domain models are in visualizing relationships between concepts, there are scenarios when we also need to dig into the details of each attribute. A data dictionary is a great technique for this.

Build Clarity with Data Dictionaries

A data dictionary is a requirements specification that provides detailed information about the individual fields that hold business data, including their meanings and allowable values. The business domain model provides a high-level view of the business concepts and how they relate to one another. In contrast, the data dictionary gets into the nitty-gritty details of the types of data stored in each field.

Data dictionaries are useful when you are updating a business process or building new functionality on an existing database, and particularly if you are migrating or integrating data between systems. If you have a long list of fields inside a use case, wireframe, or other type of software requirements specification, or if you are asking how these lists that are scattered across different deliverables work together, that's a good sign that a data dictionary will help you clarify and streamline your data-related requirements.

When building a data dictionary, remember to stay focused on the attributes that are important to business stakeholders. The point is to create clarity so the technical team can design a database structure that meets the business needs. You are not creating a comprehensive database design.

Business analysts working with a third-party or COTS application often don't have much control over the core data model. Part of the analysis process involves understanding the existing data model and how the business can best leverage the way the model stores information. Sometimes you can create custom fields for business-specific information; a data dictionary would be an appropriate way to capture those requirements and be sure you aren't creating duplicate fields. If you are migrating from an existing system to a new COTS, understanding the data models for both systems and how they map to each other ensures the right information gets in front of business users in the new system (see the next section, "Data Mapping," for more details).

A basic data dictionary begins with a table that provides the simplest possible information about the data definitions in your model. As seen in figure 16, this data dictionary will identify the fields or attributes from one information source and a few critical pieces of information about each attribute.

Figure 16. A data dictionary for instructional software

Field Name	Required	Type	Field Length	Notes
Course Name	Yes	Text	25	
Course Type	Yes	List	25	Workshop, Membership, On-Demand, Self-Study, Live
Credits	Yes	Numeric	3	Can be '0' for self-study courses

Every data dictionary has four key elements:

- **Field Name –** What have you agreed to call this field? Business stakeholders sometimes use a name that's not in the physical database. There may also be disconnects between the business terminology and the field labels on a form or user interface screen.

- **Optional/Required –** Can a new record be created without this attribute? In theory this is simple, but in practice you need to understand the workflow related to a record to understand what fields can logically be required.

- **Type –** What kind of data is allowable in the field? Common types include text, date, numeric, and lists. There are also many specialty data types that include validation rules, such as email, postal code, and phone number. Types can maintain data quality and enable additional functionality. For example, if you know a field's type is "numeric," you know you can use it to search by range. This wouldn't be possible for a text field.

- **Field Length –** Is there a business-driven minimum or maximum length? Most database schemas have default lengths, so consider asking your developer what the defaults will be, or simply note any minimum that's required from a business perspective.

I also include a notes section so I can record information about how the data is created, what type of data is typically provided, or other information that doesn't have a place elsewhere.

Building a data dictionary usually generates more questions about the requirements:

- When we upload a medical form, what information do we need to capture?
- What information do we need to record when modifying an insurance claim?
- When we deactivate an employee record after terminating employment, what information do we gather?
- In addition to the information provided by an end user, what data does the system track? And what are the rules the system uses to capture that information?

Digging into each field will likely raise even more questions. For example, consider a data dictionary for a medical record that a nurse practitioner captures during a patient visit. You might start by capturing attributes for the typical assessments—blood pressure, height, weight, heart rate. Assume that these are all required fields: Does that mean the patient can't opt out of stepping on the scale? What are the implications of not capturing weight? One might be not being able to prescribe the appropriate dose of a medicine. If we want to enable a patient to opt out of stepping on the scale, could we use a weight range instead? Or only request their weight when writing a prescription? A single field like this can open up a whole new area of discussion, and data requirements often have implications for the business process and software requirements.

This seem like a lot, or like we are slowing the process down again. But much too often these sorts of detailed data questions are left to a technical professional who knows everything about the database but doesn't fully understand the business context and makes a lot of assumptions about what is needed. That is how teams end up building systems that don't work the way the business users expect.

Getting this detailed perspective on the data is a way to get clearer about what the business needs and wants so we can build the best possible system from the very beginning—or at least place the building blocks that allow us to more easily expand to our fullest vision. Whether you do this by creating the data dictionary yourself or by collaborating with a database designer to share business context, be sure the data model ultimately supports the business.

While we're on the topic, don't overlook the power of data to shift cultural and societal norms or to sustain outdated ways of thinking. Even today, all too many forms only offer two options for gender while making this a required field, leaving those who use they/them pronouns unrepresented. Many systems collect information about race, gender, and disabilities in an effort to enable demographic reporting, but I often look at the list of allowable values for race and wonder if everyone feels represented. For example, I know many dark-skinned Americans who do not identify as African American, which is often the closest choice. Similarly, many autistic professionals do not consider autism a disability, even though it's often captured as a disability instead of a general condition.

These are undoubtedly delicate issues, and political policies can impact both the data we collect and the way we organize it. The words we use matter, and so does the way we capture data. So does how we communicate when we collect what can feel like invasive personal information. I often leave demographic fields blank if they are optional, unless the organization communicates clearly about how they are using that information. I was confused by a dental form asking me all kinds of questions about sleep until I saw a note about a possible connection between sleep apnea and dental issues; after I read that, the data collection made sense.

Working through a data dictionary necessarily prompts you to zoom in on details. It's also helpful to step back and look from the perspective of the person providing information and to consider where and how each piece of information fits into the business process, what software is used to capture it, and how the captured data links back to organizational goals.

Now that we understand the basics of data structure, let's look at the analysis that supports moving data from one system to another.

Data Mapping for Data Migration and Integrations

A data map specifies how data translates from one data store to another. There are two primary types of projects that require a data map: data migration and system integration.

Data migration occurs when data is moved to a new system and the original data source will no longer be used or maintained. For example, many companies use human resource information systems, which may contain a catalog of job postings. When switching to a new system, the business may prefer to migrate the job posting information rather than rekey it.

System integration is when data is sent from one system to another on a regular basis, whether hourly, daily, weekly, monthly, or even in real time. Both data sources are maintained on an ongoing basis and the interaction between the two systems is limited to a single feed, which is typically a file in a specified format. System integrations are often built using an application programing interface (API) or extract, transform, load (ETL) processes. If someone asks for an API or ETL specification, a data map is a good place to start.

While there are nuances, any project that involves moving data will probably fit into one of these two buckets—data migration or system integration—and you can use that as a starting point for your data map.

Before you start mapping data, consider the high-level data-related decisions:

- How does the data flow? What or where is the source data and where is it going? Is the source data in one place or are you merging data from multiple sources?
- How often does the data flow? Once? On an ongoing basis? In real time?
- What source data will be migrated? Moving all records from the data source is a reasonable expectation, but it's often unnecessary and can lead to mapping challenges, particularly if there is some old, unused data.

Often you will need to speak to both business and technical stakeholders to understand what type of integration you are working on, what type of data mapping will meet the business needs, and what decisions have been made in terms of the technical architecture. Consider modeling the answers to these questions using a system context diagram (discussed in chapter 3).

The questions above are powerful even if the data migration is not automated. When my company shifted project management systems, I decided to only migrate active templates and projects and leave behind our historical projects. The automated import tool wasn't very useful. So instead of importing tasks I manually rekeyed some and delegated a few projects to other team members. The most impactful question for us was "What source data will be migrated?" (Intentionally choosing to minimize the amount of data migrated reduced our time investment significantly.)

Even when you are building automated tools to migrate data, you can save a lot of analysis and development time by limiting historical data. Always ask if the data will really be used, and for what purpose. As a rule, the more historical data you migrate, the more complex the project will be.

On the flip side, help your business stakeholders think through the implications of not migrating historical data, such as whether it will impact reporting. Objectives like reviewing history, which may be infrequent, can often be accomplished with a download that's available as needed. In the case of our project management system, knowing that original system wouldn't delete my data right away gave me peace of mind. I knew I could go back and resubscribe if there was anything I absolutely had to have.

Once you understand how the data flows and what source data is needed, you can start evaluating the specific attributes that need to be mapped and how they map over to your target data repository. The result of your analysis will look something like figure 17.

Figure 17. A data map for a website feed

Source Field Name	Req'd	Type	Notes Field Name	Target	Req'd	Type Rules	Notes	Translation
Article Title	Yes	Text	Contains HTML	Content Title	Yes	Text		
Article Category	Yes	Look-Up	Keyword	No	Text			If multiple categories, create a comma separated list
Article Content	No			Content	Yes	Text		Truncate to 4,000 characters	If truncated, back up to last full sentence and add "…

This data map shows a hypothetical map between a website's article data model (left) and a search engine's results data model (center), with translation rules on the right.

Here are the key components of the data map:

- **Source data fields.** The specific fields from your source data that will be mapped over.
- **Target data fields.** The specific fields in the target system that each source attribute will move to.
- **Translation rules.** Any data manipulation that needs to happen as information moves between the two systems, such as setting default values, combining fields, or mapping the values from one field to another.

Essentially, data mapping is about clarifying the connections between two databases and resolving potential issues. In many cases, the attribute names differ between the two systems. Even worse, the same terminology might be used to label attributes that contain different types of information. This is where the glossary, business domain model, and data dictionaries provide an in-depth understanding of how the business organizes information and what's actually in the database.

Creating a data mapping specification like this requires discovering and resolving potential issues before the mapping is implemented. You don't want to get to the point where you're trying to move the actual data between systems and all kinds of errors are popping up, or the users are reviewing a test environment and feel like their data is wrong or missing. Up-front analysis prevents a lot of those problems. Even the simple data mapping exercise shown in figure 17 can generate multiple mapping issues:

- The article title contains HTML in the source data. Would that HTML code cause errors in the target system? Would it be rendered properly?
- The source data "Article Category" can have multiple values while the search engine "Keyword" is a single text field.

This might require logic for turning multiple values into a comma or semicolon separated list in the target system.

- The article field in the search engine is truncated to 4,000 characters, while there's no limit in the source data. This could cause data loss during the migration.

Consider these other common mapping issues:

- Are both attributes required/optional?
- Are the attribute types the same?
- Are the attributes the same length?
- Do the lists or look-ups map?
- Do any attributes not have a home?
- Are there any attributes in the target system that don't exist in the source data?

In each of these cases, knowledge of the business process will help you resolve the issue. Alternatively, you may need to collaborate with the business stakeholders to discover what they're willing to invest in potential data cleanup, manipulation, organization, and scrubbing before the migration or the integration happens.

Remember that perfection is not the goal. Keep your business objectives close at hand. Decisions on how to handle an issue may involve data analysis and reporting. For example, how many blog posts are over 4,000 characters? If it's a small handful, a quick manual edit may be all that's needed. If it's most of the database, you may have a reason to advocate for a change to this character limit in the target database.

In my experience, there are layers and iterations of analysis involved in data mapping. Start at the high level, looking at the attribute mapping. Then dig into the issues and translation rules. Keep making one decision after another until you have all the details your implementation team needs to code the logic and make the data migration or integration happen. Finally, be aware that even once you've analyzed and normalized the data from a business perspective, additional complexities and nuances can emerge during the physical database analysis due to the technical structure of the data.

Remember, this is a team effort! Don't take on all the data cleanup or detailed analysis work unless no one else steps in to complete it. Do bring up issues for consideration and attention. Data issues are a common reason for major delays late in implementation, so everything you do here proactively avoids those types of issues. And since this is a team effort, let's review the roles business analysts can play in this process.

Enhance Your Productivity with Generative AI

- Upload deliverables and request a draft set of terms and definitions to put in a glossary.
- Request suggestions for data types or picklists.
- Upload data dictionaries and request a first pass at a data map.
- Upload a data map and ask for issues and suggested resolutions.
- Upload source data to analyze the scope of data mapping issues.

Business Analyst Roles in Data Modeling

When it comes to data modeling, there are a variety of roles the business analyst can fulfill.

Let's start by considering the difference between data modeling and data analysis. *Data analysis* involves evaluating the data and helping the business make data-driven decisions. This can include the ongoing use of business intelligence and reporting systems to query, report, and analyze data. Data analysis is its own professional discipline. Business analysis roles sometimes involve data analysis responsibilities because the skill sets tend to complement one another.

Data modeling, in comparison, is analysis of how the organization manages information, using the set of techniques outlined in this chapter. The data modeling responsibilities a business analyst takes on will heavily depend on the makeup of the team and the type of work.

- Is there a database architect (DBA) with strong business knowledge? If so, you'll probably review data modeling decisions and clearly communicate the new business and software requirements to the DBA so they can analyze the data requirements.
- Are you working with an outsourced development team that needs specific details? If so, you may complete a very detailed analysis, potentially in collaboration with a lead developer or DBA.
- Is there a data-savvy business subject matter expert on the team? Perhaps they can tackle some of this work while you focus on other areas of the requirements.
- Is it necessary to analyze or normalize legacy data? Then someone with specialized skills in this area must be involved, and the type of data map a business analyst would create would be a starting point, not the end point.
- Are there complex regulatory requirements around the data lineage and manipulation to consider? If so, additional technical data expertise may be required to ensure compliance.

The most important thing is to be sure that someone who understands the business and the requirements is modeling the data. The goal is to avoid anyone making uninformed assumptions on behalf of the business when it comes to how to structure and map data.

When in doubt, go back to the questions we started with in Step 1:

- What inputs will I receive before I start work?
- What deliverables is the business analyst responsible for creating for this team?
- Who reviews and receives each of these deliverables? What's the next step they take as a result of receiving completed deliverables?

Whether or not the business analyst role includes data modeling, data modeling decisions can impact other types of requirements. One of the trickiest types of projects is migration to a standardized off-the-shelf system. Often, the data structure of the new system cannot be easily changed, so most of the analysis will involve figuring out how to maximize the new data structure to meet the organization's business needs. Data modeling can quickly lead back to business process analysis. When a piece of data is handled differently in a new system, that means the process will need to change, which means that business users need to be engaged in understanding those changes and trained on the new way of doing things. (This is discussed in chapter 8, "Support Implementation.")

Data modeling can also lead to new software requirements. For example, if an attribute becomes required, that change may need to be reflected in your wireframes and use cases to ensure the software system implements this rule.

Understanding how your role fits into the context of other roles can also be ongoing and iterative work, and may change as your understanding of the scope changes. Perhaps when you first started you didn't think to ask about data modeling, but it's now clear that the scope includes a data migration or integration component. In this case, avoid unnecessary conflicts, clarify your role as part of that effort, and include that work in your business analysis plan, estimate, and timeline.

Or perhaps you've absorbed the information in this section and have decided that this is *not* analysis work that you want to do. While I've always enjoyed data modeling, I drew a clear line in my career and never learned SQL. I knew I would probably be good at it and I didn't want to get sucked into creating reports or doing any more detailed data analysis or database design work.

While you can't get away from creating a glossary, and while I feel that being able to create a business domain model is a foundational skill for business analysts, detailed data dictionary and data mapping techniques may not be the best investment of your time. Even so, you need to understand the data requirements for a successful project, ensure those requirements are completed, and be engaged in the process to ensure they are consistent with the business and software requirements. You never get off the hook completely when it comes to data modeling!

❯❯ Next Steps

This chapter covered three powerful data modeling techniques you can use to clarify the business domain and ensure that information systems capture data in a way that supports the business. It also addressed how to configure your role, and whether and when you should take on responsibility for data modeling. In today's world, understanding these techniques and skill sets doesn't just set you apart; it is essential. Here are some next steps to implement what you've learned:

- Draft a business domain model to visually model how business concepts relate.

- Build a data dictionary to capture details about the data generated through business processes and software.
- When the need arises in a data migration or system integration project, create a data map to proactively work through any data integrity issues.

Even if you don't analyze the data requirements yourself, everything you do when analyzing the business process and software requirements impacts the data. The more you understand about data and data structures, the easier it will be to identify data requirements and the more value you'll add on your project. You'll save your implementation teams loads of time managing data issues at the eleventh hour or your business teams loads of time working around bad data to use a new system effectively.

The last two chapters have focused on techniques used for software and business domain modeling and data modeling, especially during Step 5 of the Business Analysis Process, defining detailed requirements.

Eventually there will come a point when you are done. The requirements are complete. When that happens, your role doesn't end; stay engaged as the implementation and rollout unfold. But your role may not be as active as it was. At this stage, the business analyst shifts from being a driver and a doer to being more of a supporter and collaborator. It's fun to see the team run with your requirements and make them real! Steps 6 and 7 explain how you can stay involved and engaged with both the business and technology teams, and ensure the right solution is built and leveraged to generate a positive ROI. In chapter 8, we'll turn to Steps 6 and 7, actively supporting the technical and business teams to ensure the right solution is implemented. Both activities support realizing the intended ROI on the project.

8

Support Implementation

Throughout the first five steps of the Business Analysis Process the business analyst drives the show and intentionally moves the change effort forward. Now it's time for an energy shift. Once the detailed requirements are defined, most business analysts assume a more responsive and supportive role. The exception is business analysts who are filling the hybrid role of project manager.

Historically, this is where the requirements were thrown over the proverbial wall and the business analyst turned their attention to other work. However, continued collaboration throughout the implementation process realizes the value of business analysis and ensures a return on the investment in the project. No matter how complete your requirements are and how aligned everyone is while you develop them, decisions can be made during implementation, testing, and rollout that undo all the hard work to date, and the team will need your help to develop new approaches. Plus, it's natural to want to see your work through in a meaningful way. You've invested a lot of effort and thought into this initiative. You want to be sure it realizes it's intended objectives.

That's the motivation for the highly collaborative work in Steps 6 and 7 of the Business Analysis Process. Step 6 is all about supporting the technical team as they implement the solution, and Step 7 is about supporting the business team as they accept and ultimately own the solution. These are different areas of focus, but the mindset and goals are the same: to ensure the fullest possible realization of the business objectives while continuing to cultivate clarity and alignment.

This chapter will guide you through collaborating with the technical and business stakeholders to realize the desired outcomes: a successful technical implementation and business ownership of the implemented solution. You will also learn how to facilitate ongoing collaboration between the business and technical teams throughout development. As you engage in the concrete activities in this chapter, you'll build stronger relationships, learn more about the technology being implemented, and experience the joy of seeing the requirements come to life!

Support the Technical Implementation

As the development team designs, implements, and tests the solution, misunderstandings, questions, and challenges will surface. Without an active business analysis presence, technical professionals often decide on alternate approaches without input from the business stakeholders. Or, if they sense that the business analyst is no longer involved, the developers may go directly to the business stakeholder for decisions, which can introduce unnecessary complexity or conflicting requirements if the business stakeholder doesn't see the whole picture. When you stay engaged during development, you can share context with the implementation team, answer questions to clarify the requirements, explore impacts when issues arise, and ensure that decisions are revisited only when necessary. Teams that have context make better decisions about the solution design, notice opportunities, and tend to build software that business teams benefit from using.

For example, when we were evaluating new course delivery platforms for my training business, I wanted to replace our email-based feedback with a system that would let participants upload deliverables, assign those deliverables to instructors, and then give the instructors a way to provide feedback. I developed a set of business processes and high-level software requirements for this workflow. At the time we couldn't find any course delivery tools that supported the requirements so I worked with a developer on a proof of concept for a custom solution.

The moment I saw the proof of concept, I knew we'd gone in the wrong direction. It was a partial implementation of our requirements, wedded to a specific course delivery platform, and it added a ton of complexity to our workflow. We ended up investing in a third-party ticketing system instead. Participants still submitted deliverables by email, but we could manage and assign that work in a queue, which was more efficient even though it kept many manual steps. Removing the requirements to assign work to separate instructors and manage it all privately freed us to explore other readily available solutions. Today, participants upload their deliverables through an online forum, but we still receive immense benefits from the ticketing system for customer support.

I probably could have come to the same conclusion by asking for a high-level solution design instead of a proof of concept, but I was feeling stubbornly committed to building this as an add-on to our course delivery platform. In a way, I was not unlike business sponsors who make technology decisions too early or get wedded to their solution ideas, resisting business analysis efforts to first clarify objectives and explore multiple solution options. Imagine what would have happened if I'd given that developer the leeway to build out his full idea of the solution without any check-ins along the way. I would have invested a lot more money in a fragile solution that wouldn't have delivered the benefit I wanted.

With your deep understanding of the business objectives, business process, and desired software requirements, you are in an excellent position to collaborate with the technical team during implementation to help them stay on track toward the desired outcomes.

Start by reviewing the solution design, whether it's formally documented or developed collaboratively in working meetings among the software developers. Technical designers sometimes get caught up in the technical details of one aspect of the software and lose sight of other requirements. You can provide valuable input on design options while assuring that the design fulfills the requirements and supports the business objectives.

Ask to be included in these conversations. Focus on asking clarifying questions, answering questions about the requirements, and sharing context to help evaluate potential options from a business perspective. These conversations are also tremendous learning opportunities to better understand the technical environment and components in your organization, which will prepare you to involve the right technical stakeholders at the right times in the future.

While most organizations trend toward collaboration, you may still face resistance. Technical professionals understandably take great pride in their technical competence, ideas, and solutions. Be open and collaborative and avoid dictating design decisions or using these conversations to expand scope or push a perspective. If you have some technical expertise, you may need to rein in your inclination to drive the solution design or get too deep into problem-solving technical issues. Allow the team to develop their own ideas and conclusions while you provide business-focused input and ask questions.

If you don't have a technical background, you might hesitate to be involved at all. But this is a great way to learn technical language and understand how technical solutions are designed and implemented. You don't have to know how to code to know how the different systems and layers of technology work together to build an end-to-end workflow. Leverage your understanding of the software and data requirements and seek to expand your technical awareness.

On some teams, the business analyst is responsible for some of these technical activities. For example, a systems analyst or functional analyst may be responsible for aspects of the solution design. In my first business analyst role, we were responsible for something we called "data requirements" that was really a set of specs that navigated the interface between content preparation and the database design. We needed heavy involvement from the development and content teams to create these specs. Understanding the outcomes you are responsible for is critical, as is engaging appropriate stakeholders in any aspect of the technical design requirements.

Next, engage the test team by reviewing test plans and test cases. These are the final gate an implementation passes before it's released to business users, either for user acceptance testing (UAT) or direct use in a production environment. Testers also benefit from context, and while it's a great practice to include them during the final round of requirements validation, they are not always available.

As test planning begins, offer to give testers an overview of the business processes, software requirements, and data requirements while providing context for the big-picture business objectives. Testers sometimes focus on detailed nuances of the software, so it's valuable to help them understand how the business users will use the system. Share scenarios and sample data from the requirements process. Review their test plans and test cases to ensure a full traceability loop from requirements to implementation to design.

It's also common for business analyst roles to include testing or test coordination responsibilities. Once, I was hired to provide business analysis for development work to create a new product. The vast majority of technical professionals were allocated toward this new initiative. There came a point when the requirements were as complete as they could be and I found myself without another project to work on, so I volunteered to coordinate the offshore testing team. I provided tremendous value by reviewing and deduplicating defects, prioritizing defects for development consideration, and revising the test cases to make them more relevant to the business.

Filling a gap in these areas is an opportunity to demonstrate your value and grow professionally. While liaising with the test team, I built new leadership capabilities, gained experience working with an offshore team, and strengthened my communication skills. While certainly you want to take care that the opportunities you take on fit with your overall professional goals, sometimes any contribution is better than none! In my case, this testing role filled an otherwise empty time until the in-house team started tackling a few smaller change efforts.

Being available for questions helps you stay present with the entire implementation team. When technical professionals are working fast and furious to meet an aggressive implementation timeline, they may make assumptions instead of asking questions that would let you clarify, add detail, or even discover new information. When this happens, the technical solution is less likely to fulfill the actual requirements. Encourage everyone on the tech team to engage you when questions or uncertainties come up, and do your best to address their concerns as quickly as is feasible.

To be engaged in implementation, you will need to be proactive and stay aware of dependencies. Not all developers and testers will reach out to engage you. Often you'll have to encourage others to invite you to meetings, ask for updates during status meetings, and offer to be part of the development process.

Finally, proactively manage issues when they arise. As design, development, and testing unfold, issues will surface. Requirements can exceed assumptions around technical scope or be infeasible with the current solution approach. New requirements may be needed to handle system integration issues. With your understanding of the business context, you can speak about potential options on behalf of the business or, when necessary, elicit business input to make decisions. This keeps the development team focused on implementation and ensures the business is involved in key decisions, so there are fewer surprises.

But collaborating with the technical team is only part of the puzzle. A value-driven business analyst also needs to be sure the business is prepared to use the technology effectively.

Help the Business Team Implement the Solution

Even when we are focused on positive outcomes and business objectives, change is hard. And the executives with the vision usually aren't the people who have to change the way they work so a project can achieve its objectives.

Case in point: I was once brought in as the business analyst after a project was "complete." To make the organization more efficient and reduce paper waste, the technical team had implemented new document management software, customized it, and deployed it across multiple physical locations. All users had been trained on the software and were expected to use it to manage documentation related to specific processes. Then someone discovered that in one location, users were still relying on print copies for their core process. First, they would scan in newly received print documents. Then, later in the process, they would print the documents, add notes, and rescan them.

Clearly, there was a gap that kept them from achieving the original business outcomes. The new process was less efficient and used more paper. The users were understandably frustrated with the new technology because it created more work for them.

When we analyzed the process, we discovered that no one had trained the business users on how to add notes and tags electronically, or configured the system to fully support their business processes. The business users created this work-around because they thought it was necessary to fulfill the requirements of their process. We made a very small technical change, redefined the process, and trained the users on how to use the new system. The organization realized the intended outcomes.

As business analysts, we are in a great position to champion the full realization of the business objectives because we understand both the business process and the software requirements. We can empower ourselves to ensure that new technology doesn't just work in theory, but also in practice.

Start with process and procedure development. Revisit your current and future-state processes and test them against the built system. Involving business stakeholders in simulations and testing will also help identify any process gaps. You may also want to develop detailed step-by-step procedure documentation that can be used in training new users.

Next, consider training. Up to this point, you've likely involved select stakeholders. Now is the time to train all end users on the updated processes and procedural changes. Identify who requires training and on what processes, determine what materials will be required, and decide how the training will be delivered. Your role may be to build and conduct the training or to support a subject matter expert or corporate trainer in walking through future-state processes and developing or reviewing training materials. Be sure to consider how both existing and new employees will be trained. Timing is also a factor, as final training materials often cannot be created until the final technical solution can be reviewed.

Implementing process changes will often require changes to organizational assets such as email templates, forms, contracts, legal

documentation, help files, customer support FAQs, and system documentation. You may be responsible for identifying which assets need
to be updated, updating the assets, or overseeing the changes.

Another consideration is user acceptance testing (UAT), the testing
of working software that's completed by the business users to ensure
it meets their needs. Involve the business stakeholders for UAT at the
best possible time—early enough to have an impact on the delivered
implementation but not so early that testing is roadblocked by stability
or technical integration issues. Business analyst responsibilities during
UAT can include clarifying test objectives, developing test scenarios
and scripts, and identifying an appropriate set of test data. It's
common for the business analyst to vet and help prioritize issues
raised during UAT, weeding out minor issues from more significant
ones that impact the business objectives. The "Technique in Focus"
section later in this chapter explores how to combine UAT and training
in a simulated process walk-through.

Another opportunity to engage is when the team is ready to go
live with the solution. While the project manager or implementation
lead will own the implementation rollout, the business analyst has
unique insight into the business dependencies and concerns. Evaluate
the rollout plan for dependencies that impact the business execution,
ensure that it includes all the business and technical components, and
be available during the rollout to support the implementation team
and after the rollout to support the business team. This may include
developing interim processes and transition requirements. For
example, when there are significant data changes, sometimes the
business needs an interim process to handle work items under the old
data model while the system is being populated with work items
under the new data model.

Once the solution is live, most business applications and solutions
require some sort of ongoing support and administration. Identify
who will do things like setting up new users and configuring options.

The business analyst can also help by clarifying what types of post-project requests fall under ongoing support and which would be new features or projects requiring a full team.

Your organizational environment will also play a significant factor in your role and expectations across all these possibilities. Some larger and more formal organizations have entire departments dedicated to training and change management and schedule out significant time for the rollout and postimplementation support. Smaller or less formal organizations may barely pay attention to these areas and assume the business stakeholders will take responsibility for implementing the change. Often, barely managed chaos ensues directly after the technology deployment unless the business analyst plays an active role in this step.

No matter what responsibilities you fulfill, this is an exciting time. You get to see all the work you've done become a living reality. And while it's an exciting time for you and the implementation team, it's often filled with anxiety for business users, particularly when they aren't prepped for the change or are resistant to it.

Being available and actively sharing all you've learned and developed so far can help smooth the transition and strengthen relationships that you'll leverage in the future. Still, be careful not to take on too much. The less you own directly while still ensuring the business is implementing the solution appropriately, the more you help the business users embrace change and own the solution themselves.

Develop Current-State Documentation

As you collaborate throughout the implementation and manage change, there is one active piece of work for you to do: document the current state. The current state includes all the business processes, software requirements, and data models that are implemented as a result of every project, initiative, and ad hoc change implemented in this organization up until now.

Current-state documentation provides a jump start to understanding the organization and its technology and processes, for you or any other business analyst working on an effort touching the same processes and systems. It also provides reference material for those responsible for maintaining and supporting the system. Despite these advantages, most teams do not have access to current-state documentation. This makes starting a new project and getting a handle on a new area of the business much more challenging than it could be.

In my experience, proposing a separate initiative to create current-state documentation has not been well received. (I'm so passionate about current-state documentation that my very first consulting package was focused on this type of work. I never sold a single package!) It not only requires the business analyst's time and investment, it also requires discovery, analysis, and validation with both business and technical stakeholders, and it can be difficult to justify pulling their attention off active projects to focus on documentation.

Instead, I've found the most success in leveraging new requests and initiatives as opportunities to build current-state documentation relevant to the work at hand and collaborating with motivated business end users and the occasional developer who will slice away an hour here and there to explain how things are built.

Every project is an opportunity to build out pieces and parts of the overall system documentation. And as you work on one change after another in the same area, you can experience the efficiencies of referring to your own documentation and add to it over time, rather than starting from scratch.

Even though you may face resistance, this work adds a lot of value. Business analysts who worked in the same company after me have reached out to thank me for the documentation I'd left behind because it helped them be more effective. Even though it was most likely outdated, it gave them a starting point. Quick tip: Always add your name as the owner or author so you get credit where credit is due!

As we begin to leverage generative AI as part of our discovery and analysis process, having assets that document the current state will enable us to run scenarios, construct future-state models, and run impact analyses in more automated ways. As our organizations grow more automated and complex, current-state documentation will become even more valuable.

Revise Requirements and Manage Changes

I've never been part of an initiative where every requirement was implemented perfectly and then elatedly accepted by the business. Something *always* changes. The business will discover issues during UAT that impact their day-to-day operations, or a competitor will release a new offering that shifts the priority of various features. The development team will run up against feasibility issues or system constraints and need to find alternate solutions, or will simply run out of time to implement all the requirements. As much as we want to work to minimize unnecessary change, reduce expensive rework, and ensure the business objectives are realized, change is normal and a certain amount of change is to be expected throughout the course of an initiative.

A "change" in this context is any modification to the requirements that shifts expectations for the project. In an agile organization, changes may simply be new items added to the product backlog and addressed in future planning sessions. In organizations that do more up-front planning, changes may impact scope of any of the detailed requirements deliverables.

When it comes to change, understand what you are managing and why. What is the shared understanding you've created up to this point? What expectations have been set, and with whom? Why are those important in the context of the project and larger organizational priorities? What are the consequences of the proposed change?

The first business analyst I hired once told me that there is really no difference between a change and a requirement. They are just two different views on something that needs to happen. This way of thinking normalized changes for me. Changes are just requirements that surfaced on a different timing than we may have preferred.

A change shifts expectations, and that requires communication. No matter how your organization defines change, you need a process for acknowledging changes, validating or approving them, incorporating them into the requirements and implementation plans, and communicating about the impact.

Many more formal and traditional organizations have a change control process that's designed so that someone approves significant changes affecting the scope, business objectives, schedule, and/or budget. That process tends to be rigid and change-averse, which is why the phrase "change request" tends to be distressing to the business sponsor who will need to handle the associated impacts. But a formal process is not always necessary. Many of the changes that surface during implementation can be handled with communication, negotiation, and updates to the requirements deliverables. Even without a formal change control process, you might be responsible for scoping the change, assessing its business impact, and creating a plan or estimate for incorporating it into the detailed requirements.

Context always matters. For example, timing impacts the scope of a change. The earlier a change is identified, the easier it is to address it. Changes that surface toward the end of a big effort tend to be more expensive and difficult to incorporate. It also matters who the change impacts. For example, when you are working with a third-party development team or vendor, change often has contractual implications because it impacts previous commitments to a certain scope of work within a specific timeline and budget.

While there are many nuances, there are two major types of change: new or changed requirements and deleted or deferred requirements. New requirements are changes that add to the scope. These often come from the business team. Deleted or deferred requirements are changes that reduce the scope, often with the goal of meeting budget and/or timeline constraints. These often come from the technical team.

Let's consider new or changed requirements first. Here are some questions to ask to investigate the change:

- What's the business justification for this change?
- Who is asking for this change and why?
- How does the change impact other requirements or aspects of the solution?
- What's the full scope and impact of the change? (Keep in mind that the impact may occur outside your team.)
- Is this really a change, or is the requirement simply met in a way that the business isn't expecting? (Many changes, and a lot of defects, can be opportunities to tweak the business process and improve training.)
- Who needs to be part of deciding whether or not to move forward with the change?

Often, you'll need to assemble a small team to collaborate to understand the change, the impact, and the solution possibilities. In some cases, even pulling this team together could be a distraction from work in progress, so you may have to defer the analysis if the change is not truly a priority. This means you may need a gateway or prioritization process before detailed analysis on a change even happens.

If the change is not approved, it can be put on hold for a future phase or project. If it is approved, it's incorporated into the delivery. This means updating all the impacted requirements deliverables and communicating those changes with anyone who is affected.

Now, let's look at deleted or deferred requirements. Here are some questions to ask to investigate a change that would delete or defer a requirement:

- What is the root cause of the issue?
- What specific requirements cannot be met and why?
- What assumptions are we making about the requirements or business objectives?
- What are the other possible ways we can achieve the business objectives?
- What possible work-arounds could we put in place while we deal with this limitation?
- What would it take to honor the original requirements? (Options often include more time, more budget, or negotiating other requirements.) Is the business willing to consider those trade-offs?

Often, deleted or deferred requirements can be handled within the team or approved by the business sponsor. For example, on my first project, we had a must-meet timeline and it was understood that not every requirement would be met. As developers worked through implementing individual use cases, they would bring me issues and constraints. I had a direct line to the product manager who would make decisions and approve changes. I updated deliverables and regularly communicated with the entire team about the updates. We ended up delivering a strong core product close to the originally hoped-for date.

However, handling deleted requirements can become contentious, particularly if the organizational process and culture dictate that an approved scope involves a commitment from the team. The business sponsor and stakeholders may want to know why the team's understanding of the implementation changed, and it may seem on the surface that the technical team is focused on other priorities or is not putting enough effort into the implementation for other reasons. This is when change starts to get associated with blame and often leads to frustration. Multiple significant cuts in scope can be difficult for business stakeholders to accept.

The reality is that we only know so much during the scoping process. There are many technical unknowns, and even detailed unknowns, when it comes to the requirements. Ideally, a project manager is helping the team identify, manage, and mitigate risks, which provides more context for technically driven changes.

Technical complexity and the level of skill and experience with the solution option are also big factors. By way of analogy, consider two different kitchen updates. Imagine updating a small kitchen in an older home: You could go into it with the objective of replacing appliances and cabinets, maybe even moving a wall, and expecting there would be some flooring and electrical work. An unexpected finding, like dangling wires and uneven ceilings and floors could significantly increase scope, time, and cost. In contrast, a remodel on a newer, larger home might involve just refinishing cabinet doors and replacing the counters, sink, and appliances. Although the job is larger in terms of square footage, it's significantly less complex and involves much less opportunity for unexpected work.

It's similar with software. When you are working with known existing systems, it's easier to provide estimates and reduce risk, because a lot is known. When making bigger changes, you introduce the possibility of unknown impacts, and your plan becomes more tentative. The same thing happens when building and integrating new solutions. Every component, system integration, and requirement adds complexity, and that complexity increases the risk of the unexpected which leads to change.

As technically driven change surfaces, help the team craft a story and explain what happened. Try to navigate the team away from blame and into positive solutions. Call attention back to the business objectives and keep them top of mind as you navigate potential options. Focus on leveraging the time and budget you have to deliver the most possible value to the business while encouraging positive relationships between business and technical stakeholders.

Handling change well and managing expectations helps maintain healthy collaboration and connection, particularly between business and technology stakeholders. Any investment you make to keep this process positive and collaborative will pay dividends.

A forward-thinking, value-driven business analyst will plan for a certain amount of business-driven change toward the end of the project. While you're defining future-state business process models and helping formulate training plans, additional ideas will surface about how to improve the technology solution. Once an end user sees exactly how they will be using a piece of software, they almost always discover something wrong with it. Sometimes business stakeholders don't see the full possibilities until the initial solution is in front of them.

While you want to minimize these changes through the discovery, analysis, and validation activities, it's nearly impossible to eliminate them completely. Small changes, such as user interface adjustments, might not surface until the final user interface can be reviewed. Larger changes, such as how an end user navigates between screens, may not be apparent until the future-state business processes are defined. Other changes can surface if decisions are made during the technical design and implementation without consulting the business stakeholders.

Whatever change surfaces and however it comes about, use your detailed knowledge of the business and project context to understand the value, analyze the impact, and help both business and technical stakeholders make their case for issues that need to be addressed, whether to realize the intended business objectives or to meet a deadline or budget constraint.

Enhance Your Productivity with Generative AI

- Research technical concepts and components so you better understand the system design.
- Update organizational assets, including current-state documentation.
- Assess the impact of a proposed change request.
- Identify risks in the rollout plan.
- Generate test cases and UAT test scripts.
- Draft step-by-step procedures from future-state process models.

▶ Technique in Focus: Simulated Process Walk-Through

One technique I wished I'd learned earlier as a business analyst is a simulated process walk-through, which combines aspects of process/ procedure development, training, and asset updates. I stumbled across this technique almost by accident, when the project manager on an internal business system update recognized that we had a group of technology-resistant stakeholders who would need some extra hand-holding to make the rollout a success.

The implementation was being managed in an agile way, so we had access to new working software in a test environment every two weeks. Once a critical mass of functionality was ready, I traveled to do the first walk-through in person. Subsequent walk-throughs were virtual, with the users sharing their screen as I talked them through the process. It goes like this:

- Give users access to a test environment, ideally one with relatively recent data.
- Choose a process to walk through.
- Ask an end user to use the test system to complete the process. You might demonstrate the process first, and may talk the user through the process, but you get the end users actually using the system.
- Watch for hiccups and challenges, identifying training issues, usability issues, and true defects.
- Repeat this process with new scenarios until each end user has a chance to execute the new process in the test system.

This approach works well for a smaller team where everyone can participate together and each person take a turn at the keyboard. For larger teams, you could break into groups, first training one set of stakeholders and then having them train the others.

Remember that the first time using a new system and executing a new process is always awkward. Whether that first time is in production while executing time-sensitive work or in a test environment on sample data, there will be a learning curve. The simulated process walk-through is a great technique to work through that learning curve early on so that the actual rollout goes much more smoothly.

✓ Success Strategy: Manage Technical Delays

One of the most difficult challenges to navigate is the almost inevitable changes to the technical implementation timeline. Especially when the initiative is large and complex, the technical implementation is difficult to plan and manage with accuracy, and this makes it difficult to manage the timelines for the responsibilities you and the business stakeholders have. These scenarios are common consequences of timeline slips:

- Business stakeholders allocate time for UAT but the application is unstable and they can't complete any of their test cases.
- Trainers begin to create materials but are unable to capture final screenshots for their procedural documentation.
- A significant technical design change, made to accommodate scheduling concerns, impacts the future-state business processes.
- Even nonissues can appear to be technical oversights, such as a specific integration point not being available during testing because it's scheduled later in development.

As issues like these come up, the business community can get understandably frustrated and begin to distrust the technical team. They tend to log complaints and issues reflecting what they are seeing in the test environment. Meanwhile, the members of the technical team are working overtime to deliver a solution and feel their work is unappreciated.

You can help maintain strong positive relationships between these groups by communicating as much as possible as often as possible. When there is a technically driven change, explain this to your business stakeholders in a way that speaks to their perspectives as well. When there are issues with the test software, help find work-arounds and communicate them to the business, explaining how the implementation plan impacts what's currently available and not available. When feasible, delay their involvement while the technical solution is unstable.

One of the often unstated aspects of the business analyst role is cultivating and protecting a positive relationship between your business and technology stakeholders. These relations pay dividends as the implementation progresses and on future projects involving the same people. Your ability to see the big picture and communicate well with everyone involved helps in managing expectations and maintaining relationships.

This is not so much a responsibility as a mindset, and the mindset is certainly not isolated to this stage. It's an ongoing way of working to break down communication barriers and build trust. But in this stage, outside pressures often exacerbate mounting internal tensions, so any time and care you take to appreciate everyone's perspective, manage expectations, and repair any breakdowns is well invested.

This contribution is not just for the team but also for you. Your credibility is on the line. You've worked hard to build trust with stakeholders, and as you've gained buy-in on one process change and one software requirement after another, you've built a set of expectations. You'll probably be working with these team members again, whether on this initiative or a new one. And even if this is a contract or consulting gig, your reputation follows you. You can't control the outcome, and you ultimately don't own the solution, but you can do your best to continue to create clear pathways of communication and keep everyone on the same page and focused on the best possible outcomes.

✔️ Success Strategy: Enable the Business to Own the Solution

We've been building up to an essential success criterion, not just in this chapter, but throughout the entire book: enabling the business to own the solution.

As a business analyst, you will eventually move on to another project, another program, or another area of the business. Even if you are embedded in a product team or a value stream, your work is in change and evolution, not the day-to-day. In contrast, the end users, department leaders, and executives will work with the delivered solution until the next change initiative. At some point, you need to step out of the way and let them take the lead.

While considering all the possibilities we've discussed in this chapter, remember that you can add just as much value by facilitating key aspects of the process, from UAT to training, as you can by doing this work. Watch for stakeholders who are stepping into leadership roles and support them. Whenever possible, be a reviewer and adviser, provide advice and encouragement, and help them problem solve issues. Be a resource and a go-to person, not the person who is running the show! Ultimately, you want the business, in partnership with any ongoing technical support they might need, to own the solution.

If this sounds challenging, envision what your day-to-day work will look like if you don't transfer ownership:

- Business end users will come to you daily asking how to complete their regular tasks.
- You will get bogged down in an endless stream of defects and change requests.
- You could even become immersed in a systems administrator or applications role, providing ongoing support such as setting up new users, configuring options, and adding new fields or workflows.

None of this is wrong per se; it's essential, value-creating work. But it also keeps you stuck in one area of the business working on ongoing maintenance. Your skill set and talents offer much more value working on more significant initiatives and changes.

Like managing technical delays, this is a mindset more than a task. It starts when you identify key stakeholders, continues as you clarify business objectives, and sweeps through the entire initiative as you gain alignment and clarity around the desired solution. Once the desired solution becomes real, the business owns using it to deliver business value. Do what you can to step back while staying actively engaged.

❯❯ Next Steps

The message of this chapter is to ensure that the initiative realizes its intended objectives and that decisions made after the requirements are "complete" are aligned with business goals. Your goal is a positive ROI from not only your efforts but also the investments by the business and technical teams.

Here are some next steps to implement what you've learned:

- Analyze existing roles for UAT, testing, change management, implementation rollout, and solution design. Identify any gaps and either take ownership of them or work with your project manager, business sponsor, and/or implementation manager to fill them.
- Start building relationships with colleagues in these roles and preparing them for the change ahead. Set up your availability as a go-to person for questions, feedback, and validation, and create a plan to check in with them as the implementation unfolds.
- Identify where you personally can make the most impact and what responsibilities you may want to explore taking on as you navigate the bigger picture of your career.

- Consider your calendar and commitments. Does this work fit into your current priorities and align with management expectations? Do you need to make any adjustments?

Again, these steps are all about realizing the intended business objectives, staying in scope, and ensuring the decisions made early on aren't revisited and rehashed unnecessarily.

Once the implementation is complete, value creation can begin! And that leads us to the eighth and final step of the Business Analysis Process: assessing the value created by the solution.

9

Assess the Value Created by the Solution

If you are implementing all the Business Analysis Process steps in your real-world work, you'll have accomplished a lot:

- defining business outcomes,
- working through details,
- solving problems big and small,
- building and strengthening relationships,
- managing changes, and
- evolving the way the business works.

With all this activity and a focus on delivery, it's easy to lose track of the big picture. Why are we making all these changes and what value do they deliver for the organization? And perhaps even more importantly, Are we still on track? Is the solution delivering the value we anticipated?

Nothing creates more positive momentum within an organization, and credibility for the business analyst role, than a track record of successful initiatives. But if we don't stop and assess the value created by the solution, how do we know if we have a successful track record?

These questions are addressed here as the eighth and final step of the Business Analysis Process, but assessing value is a great activity to incorporate on a regular basis. You want to always be asking these questions and using the answers to guide decisions.

Since it can be difficult to remember to step back and look at the big picture while we are absorbed in nuances and details, set up regular check points. Schedule a weekly or monthly check-in with yourself or the team to revisit the intended business objectives and consider whether the project is still on track toward its goals, then make any necessary course corrections. This will not only help you stay focused but also help keep the team energized, build momentum, and ensure you are adding value every step of the way.

Still, the close of the project is a natural time to assess results, create a clear picture of the value created by the solution, and communicate these results to the business sponsor, team, and other interested organizational stakeholders. It's also a great time to reflect on the value you contributed as a business analyst and identify ways to improve your practice going forward.

Organizations fall along a wide spectrum of capability when it comes to measuring results and business outcomes. You may find yourself on either end of these two extremes:

- Your organization has no real metrics or measurements process and the idea of identifying measurable results is a foreign concept.
- Your organization has a clearly defined set of business outcomes and a robust measurement process. Measuring results is part of the culture of the company.

Most likely, your organization lies somewhere in the middle. Regardless, you can add a lot of value in this step. Assessment doesn't have to happen all at once. If your organization is immature from a metrics perspective, consider this chapter a menu of options and choose one or two to start with. If your organization is on the mature end of the scale, consider where you can make some tweaks to your process to elevate the results. There could also be opportunities to go beyond the data and look at qualitative results or add a bit of celebration to the mix.

Start by considering the immediate and long-term impact of the investment your organization just made. Look around outside the change effort and at the organization as a whole to identify tangible business outcomes created by the solution.

There are two ways to evaluate business outcomes: quantitatively and qualitatively. A *quantitative* evaluation involves using measurements and data to assess the value delivered. A *qualitative* evaluation includes an abstract evaluation of the value delivered. Let's start by taking a deeper look at quantitative data.

Make Quantitative Assessments

Quantitative reports show the measurable results that directly or indirectly tell a story of the tangible improvements made in your organization. To conduct a quantitative assessment, you'll need to gather data from a defined timeframe both before and after the solution implementation.

I've worked with a lot of smaller companies with informal practices, where measuring results was simply not a focus. But I consulted on one project where measuring results was a priority. The goal of this risky, uncertain project was to migrate customers from one product model to another. We split the project into two phases, starting with a pilot set of customers, and conducted a comprehensive review after the first phase before moving onto the second.

The project goal was to migrate as many customers as possible to the new model. Customers were divided into two groups that received different email campaigns. To quantify our progress, we first looked at the data by customer, and then rolled up this data to evaluate the total revenue generated and the conversion rate (converted customers / total customers). We didn't have an automated way to segment the sales that could be attributed to this work, so the sales manager manually identified sales and created a detailed sales report. Automated reporting is not always necessary!

We also evaluated the campaign results by looking at distribution, opens, unique opens, clicks, unique clicks, and click rate for each email in the campaign. These data points helped us see how many existing customers we were reaching, and added more context to the sales conversion numbers. With this data, leadership was able to make more informed decisions about phase 2 and rolling out the new product model to all customers.

When considering what data to evaluate, aim to measure the ultimate business outcomes as well as data points that support those outcomes. In my example, the ultimate business outcome was to generate revenue and convert as many customers to the new model as possible. The open and click rates on the delivery campaign were data points that support those outcomes, as these indicated how many potential customers saw the offer. Some potentially richer supporting metrics, although more difficult to track, would have included customer inquiries about the new model and on-page tracking (such as hovering over the "convert now" button but not actually clicking it). Here are some other data points you can consider:

- number of new leads
- number of sales
- number of repeat sales
- number of orders
- revenue
- profit
- issues reported
- issues resolved
- customer praise

- refunds
- failed payments
- cancellations
- inquiries
- total effort (in minutes, hours, days, for a specific task or process)
- duration (again, for a specific task or process to be completed)
- transactions (these can be specific to your domain, for example: claim, booking, appointment, payment, filing, registration)

For the sampling of mission-based objectives we discussed in chapter 2 (under "Make the Business Objectives Clear"), you could measure:

- carbon released or sequestered
- waste created, eliminated, or recaptured
- energy consumed
- number of people represented from a specific group
- dollars allocated to community programs
- accessibility ratings
- professional development hours

You can also make these metrics more specific. For example, instead of "Issues Resolved" you could report on "Issues Resolved within the SLA" or "Issues Resolved by Level 1 Support." You could also look at any of these data points in comparison to another data point to gain deeper insights. Consider the following possibilities:

- sales per salesperson
- orders per fulfillment representative
- issues reported per customer

- revenue per employee
- ratio of new sales to new leads
- ratio of positive customer emails to total number of customers

The possible data points are limited only by your imagination— and, of course, your organization's data collection and reporting capabilities.

Even if you don't have actual data, you can use these types of metrics to start to tell a story about the changes. What metrics do we anticipate improving? What does an improvement look like? What's our justification for believing the solution will impact this measurement? What can we measure that supports these claims?

There are also metrics that make sense to capture within an initiative, but not holistically. For example, in our monthly reporting at Bridging the Gap we capture our average open and click rates across all emails. We watch this baseline month-to-month and identify potential issues, such as our email deliverability going down. Within a promotional campaign, we evaluate the open and clickthrough rate of each email to identify the types of content that resonate the most and impact sales.

When first pulling together quantitative data, start with data your organization already collects. Evaluate the possible data points and see if any would be directly impacted, and how you could use the available data to show the impact of the new solution. This can be difficult, as metrics can often be affected by many factors, some of which are external to the business. The solution could have a positive impact even as the metric itself goes in the wrong direction for other reasons. Historical trends and additional tracking specific to the solution are ways to show the actual impact.

Next, identify data points that would tell a more complete story, even if your organization does not currently collect them. Consider what it would take to collect and report on these measurements. Sometimes a measurement can be manually collected and/or reported for a specific duration to create a baseline and analyze the impact. Other times, it may make sense to incorporate collection and reporting into your organization's ongoing business processes. Collaborate with your business stakeholders to identify appropriate metrics, collection mechanisms, and reporting schedules.

As your organization matures its ability to measure results, you'll want to begin discussing measurements while defining business objectives. Ideally, each business objective is tied to one or more tangible measurements that show the business outcomes, and at least a few supporting metrics that can show short-term momentum. That way you can begin collecting data on the current state before the initiative even starts, so that once the solution is implemented you'll be able to track progress and show the precise impact of the solution.

As powerful as quantitative assessments are, they are not always possible and do not always tell the entire story. It's always a good idea to consider qualitative measurements as well.

Make Qualitative Assessments

Qualitative assessments are more abstract, and capture information that is not easy to measure in quantifiable ways. Even if you've identified a few potential quantitative measurements, I encourage you to go deeper and identify some qualitative outcomes too, as they often bring a richer context to the statistical results. And if you aren't in a position to identify quantitative measurements, qualitative is a great place to start!

Many organizations, even much larger ones, simply don't have baseline data to compare against in easily accessible and measurable ways. As much as we might want to measure results, doing so could require more effort than the change itself, not to mention an organization-wide culture shift. If your organization does not typically assess the value created by the solution, these are excellent first steps to articulate the value created by the work you and the team have completed.

Here's an example. I recently signed up for a new service with a local composting company. The company didn't appear to use much online technology and the process unfolded as follows:

1. I submitted an online web form to request a new service.
2. I received a call two days later to tell me about the service and confirm interest.
3. After following up, one full week later I received a PDF contract and electronic debit form that I had to print, sign, upload, and send back via email.
4. Another full week later, I received my bin and was able to start saving materials to compost.

Now, imagine if the organization made this a web-enabled process: providing information about the service and pick-up schedule online, eliminating the phone call, and enabling a new customer to sign the contract and set up their service independently. A company like this isn't likely to be able to quantify how much human effort is involved in managing new customer onboarding, the average time lag between receiving a new customer's request and getting their service set up and running, or even how many potential customers get lost in this process and never become customers at all. However, they could clearly articulate qualitative results:

- Eliminated several manual steps that required extensive effort from the internal team.
- Sped up the customer onboarding process, decreasing the time between the expression of interest and starting service.

- Potentially rescued many lost customers along the way due to lack of available information on the website, time lag between steps, and complexity of the process.
- Catered to a wider, younger potential customer base that is more likely to sign up for services online.

Even with these qualitative benefits realized, it would be important to watch the data and support boxes for the first days and weeks, ensuring customers continue to sign up at an acceptable rate, monitoring for customer service issues, and reviewing website analytics for any unexpected drop-offs. Then, within a few months, we could measure the number of new customers and run a comparison to confirm that the result is truly positive.

Consider the following ways to showcase the qualitative results from your project:

- **Tell a story.** Write a few sentences describing the before and after. Screenshots of the new system (or comparing the old system to the new one) can enhance your story.
- **Identify efficiencies.** Identify the number of manual steps and handoffs that were automated, shifted, or eliminated completely. You can show this by using a high-level process map (see chapter 2 under "Technique in Focus") and color-coding the steps that were eliminated or optimized.
- **Secure testimonials.** Capture any feedback from customers and end users showing how they feel about the new solution and its impact on their work or perception of your company.
- **Use a System Context Diagram.** Use this model from chapter 3 (under "Technique in Focus") to show the new system integrations that created value or the integrations removed to simplify the technical architecture.

As you consider qualitative outcomes, be sure to take into account unexpected side benefits:

- **Foundational work**. Does any part of the solution establish a foundation for future initiatives? For example, in my first project, we connected our online content products to a backend system that focused on managing customer data related to print book sales, enabling our company to explore alternative business models.
- **Roadblocks and challenges.** What technical and business issues did you work through and how could those support future projects and changes? For example, once the composting company automates the customer-facing process, the data and tools might be ready to support analyzing and optimizing driving routes and schedules.
- **Team collaboration.** How did the team break down barriers between departments or heal strained relationships between business and technology teams? On one project, we engaged a business department that had previously been disempowered and helped them be part of a positive organizational change, creating momentum for future initiatives.
- **Improved performance and code cleanup.** Did you eliminate any outdated code or functionality? Reduce technical debt? Make tweaks to improve performance?
- **Simplification.** If you simplified a business process or eliminated manual work, how can that effort be repurposed into more meaningful and value-creating work?

Hopefully this gives you a lot of ideas about how to articulate the positive outcomes. But if you are still stuck, here are a few more questions to consider:

- What changes were implemented? Review your process models and requirements artifacts to list each change. Then ask, What was the positive outcome from each of these changes?
- As you consider each change, dig deeper and ask, Why is this valuable to the business? What does this change enable that wasn't possible before?
- What will the business look like in three months, six months, one year, or even three years because of these changes? How has the vision of the future changed?

If business objectives were never identified clearly or in a measurable way, it's impossible to measure the results against them, but that doesn't mean that value wasn't created. Articulating that value is a great way to start paving a path toward discussing business objectives in the future.

Finally, as much as possible, articulate the benefits in business language and in terms of business value. Software and data requirements are necessarily deep in the technical weeds. Why would a business user care about these changes? What impact would a business leader value? How do these changes support your organization's goals, strategies, and annual plans? Keep digging until you discover some possibilities.

Communicate the Results

Now that you appreciate the outcomes created and can describe them in qualitative and/or quantitative terms, share this information within your organization. Here are some communication techniques to consider:

- Distribute a report via email or your team messaging system.
- Hold a lunch-and-learn where you report on the results,

perhaps with the business sponsor. (Consider combining this with a success party and provide lunch, coffee, or treats.)
- Fold the report into other communications, such as a monthly, quarterly, or annual report to executives, board members, or the monthly company newsletter.
- Announce the results on the organization's intranet.
- Include the results in the retrospective.

Sharing positive results is a great momentum builder within an organization. Everyone likes to do work that matters. Reporting on outcomes ties each person's contributions to the organizational strategy. For those business users who were part of the change effort, seeing the tangible outcomes from the transition they made validates their effort and can improve engagement on future initiatives.

This is a great time to shout out everyone involved. Highlight the business stakeholders who participated in the requirements discovery effort, the technical professionals who built the solution, the business sponsors who funded the project, and the end users who are now using the new solution. Everyone wants to feel valued and appreciated. If it's not appropriate to share these recognitions publicly, reach out privately to express your appreciation.

This is also an opportunity to plant seeds about follow-up projects and initiatives. Scoping and analyzing the requirements brings so many new ideas to light, and many get sent to a parking lot for an eventual phase 2. You may also find that while your project created some positive business outcomes, there are still some gaps to achieve the intended goals. If appropriate, use these communications to suggest the next set of enhancements to get even more value from the original investment.

As you might realize, a side benefit of assessing the value created by the solution is that you will never be out of work. By analyzing the value created by one initiative, you start the cycle on a whole set of new possible projects, all of which will need your time and expertise as a business analyst.

Keep in mind that you don't have to wait until the end to communicate positive results. One way to sequence the detailed requirements work is to focus on quick wins. When you do so, be sure to celebrate those wins! Even without quick, measurable wins, you can share qualitative results like foundational work, improved relationships, and improvements made as part of clarifying current-state business processes. Be on the lookout for the value that's created throughout the project, and share those wins as visibility and publicly as you can!

Enhance Your Productivity with Generative AI

- Request measurements to quantify business objectives.
- Share previous and current state and ask AI to draft a story, highlight key points, or create a visual showing the value created.
- Upload data generated by new processes and ask AI to quantify or add structure to the results.
- Upload a retrospective or notes and ask AI to draft a slide deck to present the results or create a short executive summary.

✔ Success Strategy: Embracing Change When Reducing Headcount is the Outcome

As much as I value celebrating wins, recognize that business outcomes are not always positive for every individual. Sometimes positive change means shifting roles and reducing headcount.

I once helped implement a significant digitization and process reengineering project. Within six months, an entire office was closed and everyone I worked with was let go. I had worked hard to earn the trust of these stakeholders and help them embrace change; I had no idea this would be the outcome.

Unfortunately, this is not an uncommon outcome of business analysis work, particularly when the goals are efficiency and cost reduction rather than business growth. Digital transformations significantly shifted our organizations, and AI-enabled digital transformations will dig even deeper into previously protected knowledge work.

I certainly don't have all the answers here, but I can share some reframes to help you step back and see the bigger picture.

First, acknowledge that there's only so much you can control. Don't take responsibility for other people's actions. It wasn't my decision to close this office and I didn't have any influence over the decision. Even in a leadership position, external market factors and social, economic, political, and technological disruptions can cause shifts that necessitate unexpected responses.

Also, change creates new opportunities. By working with this group, I helped them understand their processes in new ways, see the opportunities available through technology, and learn new skills. While it didn't work out this way, this could have given them the opportunity to take on more value-creating work and redefine their contribution to the company. And our work together may have given these colleagues new skills to help qualify them for new opportunities.

Remember that there are two sides to every experience. I've also had to end contractor and employment relationships within my own business, which was even more personal and emotional. These were never easy decisions, and I was coached to realize that when a particular person or role was not working for me or my business, there was something about that relationship that was also not working for them. Each time, I could see more opportunity for the person beyond my organization than within it, and that helped me find a certain peace in my decision.

None of this is meant to be permission to participate in unethical behavior, or to encourage you to do work that's not aligned with your values. But it is important to keep your work in perspective. How can you bring awareness and compassion to your work? How can you help others be part of the positive change you want to create? How can you help others build new skills and create new opportunities, whether in this organization or the next one?

When I'm working with a change-resistant group who fears losing their jobs, I remind them that resisting the change is not going to maintain their roles. The company is more likely to value those who can be part of the positive change and explore new possibilities than those who dig in their heels and try to hold things back. Ultimately, none of us can control the future of our positions, but we can build skills, challenge ourselves, and cultivate relationships that bring us new opportunities.

When I was a manager in a company backed by venture capital—a notoriously precarious place to be—I knew I didn't have a lot in the way of career security to offer the professionals reporting to me. What I did have to offer them was new experiences: opportunities to tackle complex projects and build their skills. I took time to understand how they wanted to build their career and did my best to assign them work aligned to their career goals. Whether you are leading and managing other business analysts, or looking out for the stakeholders you come to care so much about, how can you do the same?

Finally, realize that you are also allowed to grieve. You might feel guilt for still being employed and fear that your role will be next. You might regret your participation in work that ultimately led to someone else's job loss. You might wonder what you could have done to change the outcome. You might question your leaders' decisions and wonder if you are in the right place. Your emotions are valid. Giving yourself time and space to feel and process your emotions allows you to come through challenges like these stronger and more aware.

It's OK to take some time with this. When you are ready, it helps to come back to what you can control and remember the immense value of the work you do and the positive impact your work has on your team, the project, your organization, and ultimately the world.

✔ Success Strategy: Reinforce the Value of Business Analysis

So far, we've been talking about the results from an organizational perspective. Business analysis is about improving business outcomes, and we want to focus on those outcomes. However, closing out an initiative is also the ideal time to evaluate the business analysis process itself and your own contributions to the outcomes.

There are likely ways you could have improved your contribution, and we'll get to those next. But before getting all analytical about the ways you can get even better in your role, ground yourself in what you did do.

Most business analysts I work with find this difficult. They are great at celebrating the business outcomes and the team but lost when it comes to celebrating themselves. Here's the deal: You can apply all the techniques and strategies you've learned in this book, but if you aren't fully committed to the value you contribute, the resistance you face from stakeholders will derail you time and time again. It will not only slow you down, but also cause you to doubt yourself and your abilities. You need to be 100% sold on the value of business analysis so you can effectively sell others on the value and persevere in the face of resistance.

How do you get to that level of confidence? Here's a simple yet effective practice: Celebrate your wins. Start with this project, right here and right now. What value did you create on this initiative?

There are two sides of value creation—reducing costs and increasing value. Let's look at each in detail.

Here are some ways that business analysts reduce the costs, or investment, in the project:

- **You reduce rework.** When the requirements are unclear or undocumented, or when business and technical stakeholders aren't on the same page about what the project needs to deliver at a detailed level, there is rework. Clear requirements and a shared understanding minimize rework.

- **You reduce requirements churn.** Churn happens when stakeholders have a lot of conversations about a project without achieving alignment and clarity. When you focus stakeholder effort, build momentum using a structured decision-making process that drives alignment around the business objectives and requirements, and document decisions to avoid revisiting the same conversations, you reduce churn. Consider how many emails, how many side conversations, and how much wasted time in meetings you've eliminated by bringing a structured process to the requirements. This might not be measurable but it should feel substantial.

- **You find more cost-effective solutions.** Clarifying true business objectives and analyzing the current-state process makes it possible to identify unexpected solutions that reduce or eliminate the technical implementation effort. Business process improvements often can be made without software automation; current technologies can be used in new ways. Finding alternative approaches may eliminate the need to invest in new software applications.

- **You reduce consulting costs.** When working on large or enterprise projects, organizations often hire consultants or work with external vendors, which generally come with a much higher price tag than a full-time employee. Jeannie, the program participant I mentioned in chapter 2, saved her organization $40,000 in vendor costs by mapping her organization's accounting and underwriting processes.

A huge part of our contribution is making everyone else more effective and efficient. It's easy for that value to get hidden by more visible work, like automations and code. You may never have thought about how clarifying a business process leads to efficiency-creating updates. Those wins can be so nuanced. You really have to look for them.

But cost savings are only part of the story. Your contribution also creates new value and opportunities, and maximizes the positive outcomes. See yourself as a strategic partner to the business, not just helping in the implementation of objectives, but partnering to drive growth and create new opportunities. Here are some ways that business analysts maximize the value created:

- **You discover new benefits.** When you dig into the problem or the underlying business objectives and help the business get clear on their goals, you find new opportunities and potential benefits. On one project, while observing end users working through their business process, I noticed they were copying and pasting documents into a field on a web form, and then spending a lot of time editing it. A very simple technical adjustment simplified their workflow and saved them tons of time. Where have you discovered and advocated for similar enhancements?

- **You prioritize the highest-value requirements.** When you ensure that the highest impact requirements are included in the scope, manage scope creep, and ensure each detailed requirement contributes to the objectives, you make sure the highest-value work gets done.
- **You help pause projects with a negative ROI.** While it can be difficult to recommend canceling a project, doing so can save your organization money and help realize benefits from other projects in the pipeline. The sooner you can do this, the better! The more an organization invests in an effort, the more difficult it is to pull back and redirect the team to more valuable work.
- **You help the business leverage solutions.** Your work doesn't end with the software. You also help the business leverage that software effectively. Because you see both the business and solution perspectives, you bridge a lot of communication gaps during UAT and rollout, ensuring the initiative delivers on its intended outcomes.

Pause for a moment and get clear on this. How did *you* create value on this initiative? On other work throughout your career? What's your contribution? What difference have you made? What's possible now?

Now, consider the value you just identified. Did your statements start with "I" or "we"? I'm guessing many of them started with "we."

Most business analysts I work with tend to be entirely too humble. We tend to use "we" instead of "I" when celebrating success and "I" instead of "we" when acknowledging failures. This means we over-apologize when things go wrong and undersell ourselves when things go right. And we wonder why we our value goes unrecognized! We aren't valuing ourselves and our contributions.

The very analytical skills that make us so intelligent and give us the smarts to solve complex problems also make us perfectionists. When we turn our critical thinking and analytical abilities on ourselves, we magnify all the things we're doing wrong and overlook what we're doing right. We are great at picking things apart—especially our own abilities, skill sets, and contributions.

Another reality is that the business analyst role is inherently collaborative. We really do not get anything done independently, so the "we" statements come up first. But thinking in "I" terms doesn't mean you aren't collaborative or a team player. Asking good questions, drawing out the best in others, and helping clarify objectives for the team are actions that *you* took to be collaborative. While you worked on a team, and everyone made a contribution, *you* also made a contribution. What was it?

If you find it difficult to describe your impact, consider how the work would have unfolded if you weren't involved. How many meetings would there have been? What would the requirements have been like? What would have been implemented and what value would that implementation have to the business?

The gap left is the value *you* added. Own it.

The end of a project is the perfect time to catalog your contributions, take notes for your next performance review, and even update your resume. Right now you may be realizing how long you've been underselling your own contributions. If so, there are a few more steps you can take:

- **Catalog your accomplishments.** All the initiatives that went well. All the times you kept scope in check. The meetings where you got real work done and leveraged everyone's time effectively. The questions you asked that created insights. You can take this exercise as far as you want. I'd suggest looking back at your most recent year of professional work, at a minimum.

- **Identify your most valuable actions.** Look at the accomplishments that stand out and determine what action you took to create the result. This is where you want to think in "I" terms instead of "we" terms. What specifically did you do to create that positive result? It's easy to get caught up in pointless busy work, and this practice helps you identify the types of activities that really matter to your success. (Note: It's probably not making sure every line on a diagram is straight.)
- **Make this a daily practice.** Challenge yourself to identify at least three successes every day. They don't have to be big—they might be as simple as starting a meeting on time even though a notoriously late stakeholder was yet again late. They also don't have to feel overwhelmingly positive. Responding to a negative situation, like a difficult stakeholder comment, in a way you are proud of is still a win.

One of my mottos is "big and small, we celebrate it all." You don't have to wait for the so-called big milestones like promotions and successful initiatives to celebrate.

Celebrate feeling the butterflies as you said the right thing and saying it anyway.

Celebrate how quickly the first draft of a business process flowed.

Celebrate taking a truly rough draft of a visual model to a team meeting instead of obsessively fixing the lines when you knew it was going to change anyway.

Celebrate not checking your email for 30 minutes so you could focus on a piece of documentation.

Celebrate declining a meeting where you weren't needed instead of trying to multitask from your desk.

This might feel hard at first. We are conditioned to see what we did wrong and what didn't go well. This practice rewires your brain to look for what went right. It's totally normal if this doesn't feel intuitive or easy. Do it anyway.

For bonus points, share these wins with a friend or colleague. Celebrate each other and witness your self-esteem soar and imposter syndrome fade away. I absolutely love hearing about your successes—so please message me on LinkedIn and share!

Improve Your Business Analysis Process

Now, with your successes clearly in mind, let's turn our attention to the improvements you can make to your business analysis process and practice.

You want to be consistently improving and evolving your business analysis practice and skills so you are getting better and better at delivering business outcomes. Evaluating your own work gives you insights so you can make adjustments. While you can do this as part of a team retrospective, doing it individually allows you to go deeper and identify internal improvements. It also gives you an opportunity to incorporate feedback from the team about the business analysis deliverables and experiment with new approaches.

Consider the following questions to refresh yourself on the entire arc of your work:

- What was my role? (List all your activities and responsibilities, both the ones that were explicitly assigned and those you assumed.)
- What were my main successes?
- What went particularly well?

- What skills did I learn?
- What deliverables did I create?
- What techniques did I use?
- What types of meetings did I facilitate and attend?
- What stakeholders did I work with?
- What was the outcome?

Then, dig deep for improvement opportunities:

- What types of changes came up and when? Where these changes necessary? What could I have done to uncover these changes earlier in the process?
- What communication issues did I face? Were these issues isolated to specific stakeholders or common themes? How can I improve my communication?
- What questions and issues came up from the technical team? Did the way I structured my deliverables serve them? How could I improve my deliverables for their use?
- Did I keep the business objectives top of mind? Did we get off track? If so, why? What changes could I make in the future to help us stay on track?
- How did I come up with my best questions? What were the "aha!" moments I was most proud of? What actions led to those moments?
- Did I meet all the deadlines in my business analysis plan? If so, what contributed to my success in delivering on these commitments? If not, what issues got in my way?
- Was all the documentation I created necessary? Did I create any extra documentation or deliverables? How could I streamline my deliverables in the future?
- Did I go down any rabbit holes? Did the scope expand in unnecessary ways? What can I learn from these experiences?

- What were the biggest issues faced by the team as a whole? How could I apply business analysis skills and techniques to contribute to the solving those problems in the future?

As you reflect on these questions, you'll start to see opportunities to improve your business analysis process:

- Create a new template to repeat the success in a certain area.
- Add a new section or reminder to a template to avoid overlooking a specific piece of information that was discovered later than was desirable.
- Do away with a technique or template that didn't contribute in a positive way.
- Practice using a specific new skill when facilitating a specific type of requirements session.
- Create a meeting facilitation checklist to ensure you remember to book all necessary resources.
- Create a checklist for a specific deliverable to capture what went well in completing it and include ideas for future improvements.
- Create current-state documentation to make it easier to analyze future process changes and new requirements.
- Create a weekly or monthly check-in to look at the business objectives and make sure everything is still on track.
- Build in an alternate form of communication or remove one that wasn't helpful.

If you have the benefit of participating in a team retrospective, pay close attention to any input that directly or indirectly impacts the business analysis process, and propose changes to future projects as part of the team retrospective process.

As you identify ideas, start a list. Then consider two or three key takeaways you can take with you into your next assignment. Be specific about the change you will make and record it somewhere you'll see it often.

▶ Technique in Focus: Evaluating Potential Improvement Ideas

Now that you have a big list of ideas, you might feel overwhelmed by the possibilities. You don't have to change everything at once, and it will be impossible to implement all your ideas. Instead, start with the ideas that will give you the most impact and momentum (ideally for the least effort).

Whenever, I'm feeling overwhelmed, I like to complete a quick wins assessment (see figure 18). You can get this template as part of the downloadable Business Analyst Success Pack.

Figure 18. A quick wins assessment template

Opportunity	Impact	Effort		
Update Scope Template to include a System Context Diagram	High	Low		
Develop go-live checklist to assess business impacts	Medium	High		
Build project page with an overview of the BA role and all BA deliverables	Medium	Medium		
Replace FRD with use case list + use cases / user stories	High	High		

This template has three labeled columns: opportunity, where you list each idea you have; impact, where you rate the positive impact of making each change; and effort, where you rate the effort required to make the change.

The magic is in the two empty columns. These are up to your discretion. Consider what's important to you personally and to your organization, then identify additional criteria to represent these priorities. For example, you may want to focus on changes that impact your career, perhaps by positioning you to move into a senior or leadership position. Or perhaps your organization is moving to a value stream model or focused on scaling agile processes. You could consider how each improvement opportunity would support these organizational objectives.

And don't overlook your energy as a factor here. An idea that requires a lot of effort but that you're super jazzed about implementing will be way easier than an idea that's not too exciting.

These extra criteria are optional—impact and effort alone give you a ton of information.

Once you rank each improvement opportunity, look at what stands out. Pay particular attention to any high-impact, low-effort ideas—quick wins. These are often the most obvious places to start making improvements.

As an aside, this is a great technique to pull out during your scoping phase. You can include your business objectives as additional criteria, and list each high-level feature or idea for evaluation. This can help overwhelmed stakeholders see a big picture and decide where they want to focus first.

▶▶ Next Steps

Although Step 8 is the last step, the Business Analysis Process is circular and iterative. Assessing the value created by the solution will likely generate many ideas for future projects, product backlog items, and other work, which starts the cycle yet again!

Here are some next steps to implement what you've learned:

- Identify the quantitative measurements you could use to show tangible business outcomes. Even if you can't actually measure these data points, identify the data points you'd like to be able to measure in the future, and what you can reasonably believe about how this project impacted performance in a positive way.
- Identify additional qualitative outcomes to tell a deeper story and bring the measurements to life.
- Develop a communication plan to celebrate the business outcomes and everyone involved in generating them.
- Review the business analysis effort and identify improvements to make to the Business Analysis Process or set of practices. Put an action plan in place to make these improvements.
- Identify ways to reinforce the value of business analysis. What did you specifically contribute and what difference did that make? Capture this information for yourself and share as appropriate, at least with your manager or team.

No matter how much you might be tempted, don't let yourself off the hook with these steps! This is where you solidify the value of your role and the contribution you provide. The more you can show how successful your projects are, the more in-demand you'll be.

We've now covered all eight steps of the Business Analysis Process and many of the techniques you'll need in your toolbox as you apply this process to future projects. Before we close, the final chapter looks at how you can use these skills to grow your career—both within business analysis and beyond.

10

The Business Analyst Career Path

You are now supported by the skills, techniques, and process that we've covered over the last several chapters. You have a structured way of doing business analysis and a way to approach almost any kind of software project in a strategic and proactive way.

Now let's consider the bigger picture of what these skills and techniques make possible for you and your career. Elevating yourself and your skill set is good for you, your organization, and everyone you connect with along the way. As you elevate yourself professionally, you'll create opportunities for others to rise as well.

One of our course participants, James Dean (not the actor—he's a business analyst in Ireland), was the first business analyst at a renewable energy company. He has continually educated his company on the value a business analyst can create and the power of understanding the problem to be solved, and collaborated with stakeholders across his organization to create clarity and alignment. He's added so much value that everyone wants him on their projects, and his company is now hiring a second business analyst to help tackle all the opportunities. James has elevated himself professionally, within and beyond his organization, and in doing so he has created a new role and is mentoring a new business analyst in his organization.

If focusing on yourself and your own career potential ever starts to make you feel selfish or self-centered, remember that everything you do for you and your career has a ripple effect that expands well beyond you. Take any story I've shared in this book and you'll see it is not just about me or the business analyst. It's about the people they worked with, the team as a whole, the relationships they built, the improvements they made.

Your ripple effect is expansive. The more you grow, the more we all win.

While it can be tempting to hand over your career path to your current employer, it's essential that you take charge of your career development and career strategy. Many organizations do not have business analysis career paths, and even if yours does it may not be aligned to what you want.

Before we go any further, let's distinguish between being in charge and being in control. You don't control all the external factors. Your organization could face a significant disruption and you could lose your job tomorrow. Your project, product, or team could be defunded. You could be reassigned to a role that you thought you moved past five years ago.

But this doesn't mean you aren't in charge. Being in charge doesn't look like being in control. In charge means making intentional, purposeful choices about how to respond to external circumstances, versus reacting to them, while not allowing those circumstances to dictate your opportunities. It also looks like setting goals and taking action to move toward those goals while embracing unexpected opportunities that surface along the way. The first step to being in charge is to get really, really clear on what you want from your career. Decide what you want *before* you let external factors dictate what's possible for you.

It seems so simple, but it's not.

We're trained to choose from the readily available existing options. We look through catalogs of toys and pick one. We watch commercials and decide we want what we see.

In a career context, this looks like accepting our employer's promotion path as the default next step. And if there isn't a promotion path for business analysts (which is more common than not), we might decide that we can't be promoted as a business analyst, and focus on career growth through other titles and roles. This is totally fine if that's what you want, but it's certainly not the only option!

In this chapter, I'm going to lead you through three different ways to think about your career opportunities from the inside out (instead of the outside in): the business analyst success path, hybrid roles, and areas of focus. We'll also look at career paths beyond business analysis that your business analysis skill set can help you prepare for.

This chapter will have more questions for you than answers. I can't tell you what your career should look like, but I can help you uncover your career vision. Embrace this work with an open mind, and then take the gems that work for you and leave the ones that don't.

The Business Analyst Success Path

In my decades of work with business analysts, I've found they generally progress through the stages shown in figure 19. These stages don't represent specific job roles and aren't linked to titles or years of experience. I've seen professionals with just a few years of experience catapult into champion-level responsibilities because of their desire to support and mentor others. I've seen others stay in an earlier stage for a decade or more because they are stuck or simply content. You always get to choose. As you explore each stage, consider what elements of each stage speak to your own personal aspirations for your career within and beyond business analysis.

Figure 19. The Business Analyst Success Path

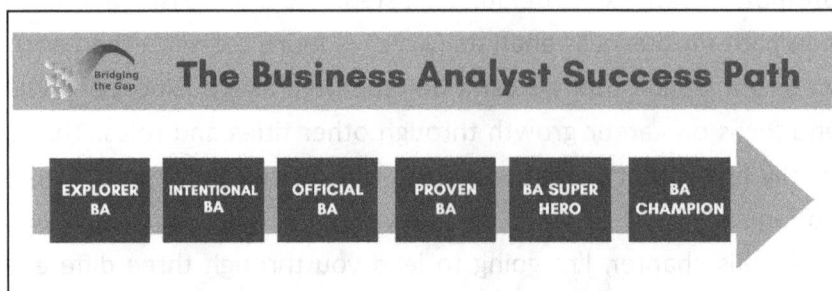

Understanding the activities, opportunities, and challenges of each stage can help you take charge of your career trajectory.

Explorer

Explorer BAs are considering business analysis as a career but are not yet committed to it. You may be well beyond this stage; after all, you've just read an entire book on the business analysis skill set! However, it's useful to revisit your career decision occasionally. Is the business analyst role really a good fit for you? What do you love about it? What don't you like so much? Have you gravitated out of true business analysis? Is it time to be more intentional about your career?

This book has given you an overview of the role, what challenges you can expect to face, and what skills you need to cultivate. Your next step is to decide—yes or no? Is this what you want professionally?

One of my favorite reviews of my first book, *How to Start a Business Analyst Career*, said, "I learned what I DON'T want to do." I want you to find a career and work that's meaningful to you and that leverages your unique set of capabilities and skills. If you discover that business analysis is not for you, that's a positive outcome from this or any book!

Intentional

Once you commit, you've moved to the next stage—the intentional business analyst. This might sound trite, but we underestimate the impact of a clear decision. When you say yes to a career path (and no to others), your next steps become clearer and more opportunities tend to surface.

It's not uncommon for someone to start exploring business analysis and realize they've been doing it for years under a different title, thereby vaulting themselves right into the proven, superhero, or champion stages. But for most people, the next logical stage is as an intentional business analyst.

At the intentional stage you are actively and purposefully pursuing a business analysis career. Many people invest in training to learn skills, and that may be why you picked up this book.

There are a few key steps to focus on in this stage (these are covered in much more detail in *How to Start a Business Analyst Career*).

Identify transferable skills. You likely have transferable skills and you probably underestimate the value of those skills. For example, a professional in a customer-facing role tends to have great communication and relationship-building skills, and knows how to ask questions to understand the problem the customer wants to solve. Consider the documents you've written, models you've drawn, and meetings you've facilitated. Even if you didn't understand the formal business analysis techniques, you may have been applying the skills intuitively. The downloadable Business Analyst Success Pack has a business analysis skills assessment you can use to create this inventory.

Start to perform business analysis techniques. Action creates clarity and opportunity. Choose any technique covered in this book and find a way to apply it in your current work, even if you are not a titled business analyst. You could start by analyzing a business process you do at work, or one you do at home. Bonus point for including a stakeholder, such as a teammate or friend, as part of the discovery process.

Seek out opportunities to be a business analyst. These can be assignments, internal promotions, lateral moves, or even a new role in a new organization. But your main focus should be seeking out business analysis responsibilities; you don't necessarily need to go through a title shift or promotion to be in your first business analyst role. And business analysis doesn't have to be your only area of focus.

Roshni Dominic is a great example of putting this advice into action. She was a support analyst at the British Red Cross when she joined The Business Analyst Blueprint® training program. She mapped the process to set up new users in her organization and showed it to a project manager, who asked for her help on a project. Roshni was able to shift her role so that 20% of her responsibilities were in business analysis. One year later, she leveraged this experience into a full-time business analyst role in a new company. Several years later, she is now championing several projects as a business analyst.

Fully acknowledge all the value you bring and start building more skills and experiences exactly where you are. Once you land your first opportunity, you are an official business analyst.

Official

In the official stage, you are in a formal business analyst role (with or without the job title) where you are responsible for using business analysis skills in your work. This could mean working on one large initiative or carving out a portion of your time on smaller initiatives. It might be a new role, a promotion within your current company, a new assignment, or even a volunteer or pro bono position.

Because business analyst roles vary significantly, you may not have all the responsibilities discussed in this book, but you will have at least some.

As an official business analyst, you will want to focus on growing comfortable and confident in the role and building your skill set to support your career growth. Here are three key steps you can take to do that.

Manage expectations. One of your most important actions in this phase is managing expectations, both of yourself and for your manager, stakeholders, and any team members. Business analyst roles vary widely and this role probably won't match up with what you've experienced elsewhere or learned about the profession. Chapter 1 covered this in depth and has tools and techniques to help you. And be sure to revisit this advice on how to clarify your role whenever you change projects, teams, or organizations.

Build credibility. Many first-time business analysts are disappointed in or confused by their role. What you read in textbooks doesn't always line up with reality. Strike a balance between using business analysis best practices to create value and staying laser-focused on the expected outcomes. You may be asked to test software or uncover requirements in unconventional ways. You may get pushback when you ask to clarify business objectives and the problem to be solved. Focus first on the foundational business analysis skills that will help you make a truly positive impact.

Apply the Business Analysis Process. As you manage expectations and build credibility, you also want to provide leadership and guidance on the different ways a business analyst can add value. Leveraging and applying the eight-step Business Analysis Process you've learned in this book is a great place to start. You've learned both the industry-standard best practices and alternatives for adding value when an organization is not yet ready for a full range of business analysis techniques and practices. Be careful not to reinvent the wheel. The same basic steps, techniques, and principles have helped business analysts across the world succeed in all kinds of industries and types of initiatives.

One of the biggest barriers I see business analysts face in this stage is perfectionism. You can't possibly get everything right, particularly when you are new to the role. Detail orientation and quality analytical thinking are hugely important, but you also want to get your models in front of stakeholders for feedback. Business analysts at this stage and the next often try to figure everything out and make a model or document perfect, failing to get the stakeholder input and engagement that's needed for true success.

Another challenge at this stage is letting go of old roles or extra hats. I moved into my first business analyst role after nearly two years as a data quality assurance engineer. It took my team a month to hire a replacement, and even though I created a comprehensive process manual about how to do the role, the new hire had a lot of legitimate questions and needed extra support to be successful. Eventually I had to set a clear boundary or risk getting sucked back into my old responsibilities and jeopardizing the commitments for my new role.

Dealing with challenges is a normal part of being a business analyst. Every challenge offers an opportunity to grow and expand your skills. As you continue to manage expectations, build credibility, and apply everything you've learned in this book, you'll become a proven business analyst.

Proven

If you're in the proven stage, you've successfully implemented at least a few initiatives with consistent results and established a solid track record as a business analyst. However, your experience may be limited to one domain or type of change effort. Your goal in this stage is to expand your experience and skill set, learning how to use new tools, apply new techniques, and navigate new project types. This is where you begin to realize the full value that business analysis brings to a change initiative.

Expand your toolbox. Leverage the credibility you've built to apply new skills and practices, ideally in ways that solve recurring project challenges and create even more value for your organization. For example, if you are proficient in user stories, experiment with some use cases to improve stakeholder engagement and deepen your analytical perspective. Add a text-based document to your business process maps for increased clarity. Experiment with a wide range of data modeling techniques to ensure the data structures support business needs.

Develop a clear understanding of your value. Practice articulating the value of business analysis in language that those outside the profession—executives, developers, business stakeholders, etc.— will understand. If you want to rise in your career, there is no space for doubting your value. Link each tool, technique, and practice you implement to the value you are creating for the business.

Seek business analysis work in new environments. To continue to grow, you need to get out of your comfort zone and experience new types of initiatives. You don't necessarily have to move into a leadership role, but you will increase your long-term career security by exploring lateral moves within your own company to work with new business applications or stakeholder teams. Alternatively, seek out volunteer or consulting work on the side. Or take the leap and shift from one company to another. Another option, as we'll address in the following sections, is to explore related roles and responsibilities from other professions.

Over my career, I switched companies three times in about five years and then tackled multiple different projects as a consultant and contractor. I learned so much from each new company and project.

The biggest challenge I faced was not my first role, but my second. In my first official role, I had the grace of my colleagues who knew it was my first business analysis assignment, the dedication of an excited 20-something committed to doing whatever it took to succeed, and a fair amount of business and technical expertise that was standing in for my unproven business analysis skills. In my second, I experienced some incredibly humbling moments:

- I got stuck in the details, not being able to sift out what was important from what wasn't.
- I had to ask for terminology to be clarified again and again, and then spent a lot of time going over my notes and models to unearth the nuances and implications of what had been shared.
- I didn't know enough to push back when the requirements got too complex.

But in addition to those humbling moments I also enjoyed several successes:

- I discovered significant areas of requirements that everyone else had overlooked.
- I helped dissolve the animosity between two technical teams by working through systems integration challenges using a business domain model.
- I made huge strides in documenting the functionality of a decades-old system that few people in the organization understood.

It takes courage and bravery to move beyond the familiar and tackle new types of initiatives in new types of domains, but it's the most important action you can take for your long-term career stability. As you stretch to expand your contribution on new initiatives, your skills strengthen and become more transferable.

When you stay in one position, doing one type of work, and get entrenched in a certain area of the business and business application, you are seen as the expert and everyone comes to you with questions. You are the go-to person for all things related to this corner of the world, which brings a lot of validation and credibility.

That might sound fantastic on the surface, but you also can get pigeonholed—seen as only "the XYZ analyst." You might even be compensated and promoted based on this expertise. Once you get to the top of that ladder, though, there may be nowhere else to go, and taking a role outside your area of expertise may feel like a step down—perhaps in both title and salary—so you only get more entrenched in your expertise. Then one day, the XYZ system gets retired, the department is shut down, and the expertise you've invested so much of your career in is no longer valued or valuable. Then you are truly stuck.

I saw this play out with one program participant, relatively new to her organization, who had invested time and effort into building transferable business analysis skills. She got a lead role on a new enterprise project not in spite of her lack of domain expertise, but because of it. The business analysts with years of domain experience were sidelined from the opportunity. They were so entrenched in the old way of doing things that the leadership didn't believe they could successfully lead the organization through a significant transformation.

I started Bridging the Gap in 2008, right around the time when technology workers were being laid off in droves. Those who had built their careers around an area of legacy expertise found it the hardest to bounce back. It's much easier to expand your horizons when you are still employed. Evolve before you have to and you'll be in the flow of opportunity instead of fighting upstream against it.

A quick sidebar here on thriving in new domains: When you work on a new type of initiative, you will often be the person who has the least expertise with the business applications, products, and domain. You'll have terminology to learn, processes to understand, business rules to clarify. You'll ask more questions and have very few answers. But your source of power as a business analyst isn't in your expertise, it's in

- the questions you ask,
- the terms you clarify,
- the models you create,
- the problems you solve,
- the objective stance you take,
- the people you align, and
- the clarity you generate.

Your fresh perspective can be just as valuable and provoking as your expertise, but you need the courage to offer it up and fail forward along the way. So if you're a proven business analyst, here are some questions to consider:

- What other types of initiatives need business analysis in your organization? How can you position yourself to be assigned to them?
- Are you passionate about a nonprofit or small business that you may want to work with (paid or as a volunteer) to expand your capabilities?
- What new business analysis techniques can you bring to your current work to sharpen your skills and broaden your experience?

- Is it time to make a bigger shift, like changing departments or even companies?
- What support do you need to feel confident in this next step? (Often this is where formal professional development and training supports to your growth.)

Keep shifting contexts and deepening your skills and one day you'll realize you are a superhero.

Superhero

Superhero business analysts are often known as the "go-to" business analysts, not just within a department but across departments. You'll know you are a superhero when people start to ask for you on their project because they trust you and your work, even when you don't know much about their area of the business. Also—and this is critically important—when you personally feel confident that you can succeed on just about any type of initiative.

If you're a superhero, you've conquered many of the obstacles you faced early in your career, and you will provide immense value and help to the other business analysts in your organization. From here, you can choose to broaden your skills beyond pure business analysis to grow into the champion stage.

Define your next-level career goal. What do you want next for your career? What would success look like? Would you prefer to lead or coach other business analysis professionals? Do you want to explore strategic work or thought leadership? Does consulting look appealing? Jot down some ideas about where you might want to go with the solid foundation you've built.

Train and mentor business analysts. You need to clone yourself so you aren't the only one who can handle all the important work. One truth I've learned through developing online training programs is that the best way to learn is to teach. You'll learn *why* you are successful as you start to share what you know and mentor others.

Establish a consistent and repeatable process. Implementing industry-standard best practices will help other business analysts in your organization succeed and enable your organization to deliver more value. This book provides a starting point you can use to build your business analysis toolbox and process.

When I teach this success path, I always ask people where they are and where they want be. While a lot of people say they want to be champions, there are always a significant percentage who choose superhero. You can continue to elevate yourself professionally in an individual contributor capacity. With good boundaries, you can circumvent the burnout. What's more, there are other paths to expanding your career as an individual contributor. There are also other career paths where you can learn new skills and expand your experience as an individual contributor. You never have to stop growing, and you don't have to be a manager to continue to advance your career.

If you got to the superhero stage without formal training, well done. That means that business analysis is your genius work. However, a lack of formal business analysis skills can also stop you at this step, because the champion stage means confidence that you can succeed and that you can help others succeed.

Many superhero business analysts have gone through our training to prove to themselves they have the foundational skill set and are ready to lead and manage others. For example, Annette had just stepped into a business analyst lead role in the Canadian government, overseeing the work of three business analysts. She wanted to prove that she knew what she thought she knew, and ensure she was setting up her team members with true industry standards and best practices. Within a few years, she was the functional manager for a large team of predominantly new business analysts with little training and career experience. Her confidence coupled with foundational knowledge enabled her to guide them to more successful outcomes and establish a strong business analyst team. The key takeaway here is that an outside perspective can help transform your intrinsic, sometimes intuitive, capabilities into a teachable, structured framework to guide and mentor a team.

Even if you think you don't want to be a champion, I encourage you to read the next section. There are many ways to be a champion, many of which are possible within individual contributor roles.

Champion

Champion business analysts help others succeed through leadership, coaching, and/or management. At this stage, you are an expert in business analysis and a champion for the role, and you support individuals fulfilling the role in a meaningful way. You see the value of the business analyst holistically and envision how it contributes to the goals of the organization. You are excited to push the profession and the role forward within and perhaps beyond your current scope of impact. You can advise others on how to best approach challenges even when you aren't in the details of the initiative.

You do not need to be a functional manager of people to be a champion business analyst. We'll circle back around to any resistance you may be feeling about being a manager, but for now, here are four ways to be a champion that may be compelling to you.

- **Management.** This involves leading and managing business analysts. In this type of role, you also elevate the awareness and value of the business analysis role in your organization. Ideally, you also create opportunities for other business analysts to advance their careers by building community, supporting others' development, and creating an organizational career path.

- **Strategic business analysis work.** Strategic work goes beyond the project level and can take the form of business architecture, project leadership, program management, or strategy analysis. By doing strategic work, you lay the foundation for successful transformations and projects.
- **Thought leadership.** This involves contributing your ideas and your best thinking to help support and evolve the profession. Your contribution may take the form of a blog, public speaking, a podcast or video channel, training, coaching, or mentoring services. It can also include contributing to a professional body of knowledge, such as the *Guide to the Business Analysis Body of Knowledge* by IIBA, or facilitating study groups or taking on leadership roles within professional groups.
- **Consulting.** Consulting at the champion level could include supporting the evolution of the business analysis practice, completing a business analysis skills assessment, or mapping out a maturity plan for a business analysis practice or project management office. Or you may complete more tactical work like turning around a failing project, leaving a team behind you to execute and leverage better practices going forward.

Do any of these opportunities sound personally exciting? Full of possibility?

While the direction you go in your career is always your choice, I believe that every practicing and passionate business analyst has the seeds of a champion within them. I also know from my experience coaching and mentoring business analysts that many of us get bogged down by perfectionism and imposter syndrome. Leadership work can feel great and necessary for other people, but not for us.

The way I see it, if you are successful as a business analyst you are already a leader. This often doesn't look like top-down leadership, because the business analyst role leads without authority. That's what makes becoming a champion a bit different. This level of work is about stepping into your authority, and that can feel a bit scary.

I get it. I had to be pushed into a management role. I was overworking and barely getting everything done. Our team had a ton of funding. I finally advocated for hiring another business analyst. I was told, "Hire one."

That's not what I was expecting, and I resisted it for weeks. I wanted this new hire to report to my manager, the CIO. I wanted anything but to be a manager. I didn't think I was experienced enough. I didn't think I could hire another business analyst. I didn't think I could oversee their work.

I only started hiring when I really didn't feel like I had a choice.

Looking back, I'm so grateful for that fateful push into the next stage of my career. It forced me to address all sorts of skill gaps in interviewing, clarifying roles and expectations, and giving feedback. It gave me incredible insight into how a manager thinks when they are hiring and scaling a team—insights I can now pass on to the business analysts I mentor.

But left to my own devices, I'm not sure I would have ever taken the step forward.

And yet I was entirely capable of building and managing that team. I hired outstanding business analysts, project managers, and quality assurance professionals, and they did amazing work. I established and oversaw meaningful processes. I built relationships with higher-level stakeholders across the company. It was all on confidence borrowed from my manager.

I preach the need for self-confidence and dedicate everything we do at Bridging the Gap to helping analysts build self-confidence because most analysts I know don't have a manager who supports them and pushes them. To move ahead in your career and do the work described in this book, you need to advocate for yourself and the value you contribute. That requires self-confidence.

So, yes, the resistance is normal, even natural. But don't mistake the resistance for truth. What's true is that you have everything you need to do this. The skills you've developed along your business analysis journey are also the skills you need to be a great leader: curiosity, shared understanding, analyzing opportunities, relationship-building, and creating alignment around a shared vision. The difference is that instead of fostering change from the ground up you are out in front, leading the way and clearing the path for others to follow. And that's a great place to be.

As you consider your work at the champion level, instead of deepening your resistance, keep asking yourself what impact you want to make.

Are you dedicated to your local geographical area, and want to be the shining light for business analysis with local professionals, employers, and recruiters?

Is your work global but focused on a specific skill area, like digital transformation projects, or a specific career stage, like starting a business analyst career?

Do you want to combine business analysis with a specialty or area of expertise; for example, training and supporting business analysts in a specific ERP platform?

Are you most excited about building the best possible business analysis practice within your organization?

In my experience, your awareness of your possible impact expands as you grow and evolve in your profession. I started Bridging the Gap intending to build a side hustle to help me stay relevant professionally while I raised young children. I always planned to go back to a "real" career in a corporate setting once they were both in school. By the time my second daughter was born, I was enamored with my training business for a whole host of reasons. I didn't want to let it go.

But what really hooked me was imagining my impact. I saw an opportunity working within one organization, shifting the culture to value business analysis and bringing in best practices. But I saw a bigger opportunity in teaching business analysts all across the world. In contributing to the development and evolution of the profession. In helping a community that tended toward perfectionism, theory, and abstract techniques by grounding people in practical, results-oriented practices. I realized I had a choice in how I continued to contribute. And so do you.

We've explored what it means to be a business analyst at the stages of explorer, intentional, official, proven, superhero, and now champion. Before moving on, consider these three questions:

- What is your current career stage?
- Where do you ultimately want to be?
- What's one next step you can take toward that goal?
  (Refer to the suggestions in your current stage for ideas.)

Career stages are just one way to look at your career. Next, let's look at the overlaps between different roles, and explore roles beyond business analysis. If you feel committed to the proven or superhero stage for now, this can be another way to expand professionally without moving into champion-stage contributions.

Unlock Opportunities in Related Roles

The business analysis skill set is relevant in a wide variety of positions, and it's not uncommon for people to leverage their business analysis skill sets while performing responsibilities in project management, software development, user experience design, information architecture, or other domains.

Historically, thought leaders in the profession have emphasized the importance of being a "pure" business analyst. This advice has been well intentioned, as there is a need at a macro level to focus on the business analysis role to establish its value across organizations.

However, at an individual level this guidance can lead a business analyst to overlook the opportunities provided by alternative roles, constraining rather than expanding the career options created by our transferable business analysis skills. The current trend is to collapse and integrate roles, meaning that each individual may have responsibilities from multiple previously distinct roles. The efficiencies and opportunities enabled by generative AI will only further this development.

I've shared a lot about my career trajectory throughout this book. I'm going to share a few highlights here, this time focusing on how my roles expanded beyond business analysis, and how those stretch areas unlocked new opportunities.

I started by transitioning from Quality Assurance Engineer to Systems Analyst, a role focused on the more technical side of business analysis work. I learned data modeling and the basics of system architecture and design, but didn't learn as much in the way of business process analysis. After moving to a new company, I was promoted to Manager, Business Analysis—a role that involved current-state analysis and program management—where I built new skills in strategic business analysis. I also oversaw an offshore testing team, leveraging my hands-on testing experience while building leadership skills.

After moving companies again, I oversaw an enterprise analysis effort across five newly acquired companies and started practices in business analysis, quality assurance, and project management, building on my experience in not just business analysis but also testing and project management. This led to a Director of Enterprise Solutions role where, in addition to managing a 15-person team, I performed strategic business analysis at a much higher level of complexity than before.

After leaving this role, I refocused on project-level business analysis work in contracting and consulting roles, leveraging my hands-on business analysis experience. I worked on several internal business applications and honed skills in business process improvement, change management, and agile practices. I started building the training company that is now Bridging the Gap, and further evolved my skills by training professionals in many different industries, functional areas, and geographical locations.

At each of these turning points, I chose to take on new challenges that were outside the traditional business analyst box. By exploring and taking on roles and responsibilities outside of business analysis, you can expand your career opportunities, grow your skill set, and cultivate new experiences to draw from as you progress in your career. Every new experience sets you up for new opportunities, many of which you may not even be aware of at the time!

While there are clear benefits to taking on tasks beyond business analysis, it can also be risky. You can take on too many responsibilities and become unfocused, find yourself doing anything for anyone, and end up stuck spinning in a dead-end role. This often means you are overcommitted and don't have the time or energy to excel.

Focus on roles that expand your opportunities and elevate you professionally. Don't take any task that lands in your lap. Be discerning about taking on new responsibilities. For example, when you are trying to get into business analysis, taking meeting notes is a great opportunity to build your listening and writing skills. As a practicing business analyst you might take on this task to help a peer, but you wouldn't volunteer for it regularly.

In essence, look for responsibilities that broaden your skill set and move you toward your career goals. If you are pursuing a business analysis leadership role, making a lateral move to project management or taking on some project management responsibilities would help you build leadership, oversight, and planning capabilities. If your goal is to become a product manager, look for responsibilities in user experience design or usability testing, join a marketing-focused project as a business analyst, or do financial planning on an enterprise project to build skill sets needed for that career.

At each step ask yourself how you can expand your options and move toward your goals:

- What related roles and responsibilities sound promising and exciting? Why?
- What activity could I take on in my current work to experiment with that role?
- What lateral moves would help me build experience to qualify for those types of roles?

We tend to think of new roles as landing points—places we will stay awhile. Instead, consider new roles and responsibilities as jumping-off points. Where will this opportunity lead? What even better opportunities will open up if you take it on?

If a particular role or responsibility will not lead you forward, then it's OK to say no to the opportunity. Also, remember that taking on a new responsibility may mean letting go of a current responsibility. In general, you want to be eliminating, automating, or delegating any task that has become boring or is no longer helping you grow.

At this point, you might feel you have more options than time and energy. If so, the next section will help you find your focus and create a sense of direction within your career.

> ### *Enhance Your Productivity with Generative AI*
>
> - Share your current responsibilities and ask for ideas to grow and expand your value-added contributions. Take it further and ask for opportunities to eliminate, automate, and delegate.
> - Use the steps suggested at each career stage, combined with contextual information about your role, project, and organization, to request specific next steps.
> - Explore opportunities to use AI to make your current work more efficient (there are many ideas throughout this book), allowing you to take on new roles and responsibilities without working more hours.
> - Share your work history and ask for a career plan that integrates and builds on all your experiences and expertise.

Find Your Focus

When people come to me feeling unfocused in their careers, it's often because they have so many options that they are confused about which one to take. Setting a 3- or 5-year career goal can feel daunting. You have no idea what opportunities will open up as you build your foundational skills, tackle more complex work, and elevate yourself professionally.

My career path looks so logical in retrospect, but I can honestly say that at the time I didn't know where each step would lead. I wasn't very intentional about it. I didn't even learn about the business analyst title until my second full-time role. I just kept taking the next step that felt right, upskilling to learn what I needed to know, focusing on contributing value, and saying yes to most of the opportunities that surfaced. This set me up on a strong trajectory, but as I've also mentioned, it led me to a place where I felt a bit disoriented. Looking back now, the only thing I would change is to step back and look at the big picture more regularly, choosing my next steps with a bit more focus and intention.

Just because you can't be sure where an opportunity will take you doesn't mean you have to chase any possibility that comes up. When you feel stuck, start with the following questions to get a sense of direction:

- Would you like to grow more in the direction of the business or get more technical?
- Do you want to be an individual contributor or do you see yourself leading and managing people?
- Do you have a passion for being a generalist and working on all kinds of projects or is there an area of expertise or specialty that's really drawing you in?
- Do you prefer long-term, full-time roles or would you like to build a variety of experiences with different organizations through contracting and consulting?
- Do you like to work with internal business applications or external products?
- Do you want to focus on specific projects and initiatives or look at the bigger picture of programs and value streams?
- Do you feel called to a specific industry like health care, energy, or sustainability?

You don't have to answer all these questions. Even two or three clear answers will give you a direction. For example, seeing yourself as a high-level individual contributor with some technical expertise would indicate that now is a great time to learn technical skills. On the other hand, an expert in a specific ERP system who wants to be a manager focusing on internal business applications would focus on applying their business analysis skills within projects related to that ERP system, learning the full range of system capabilities, and building their leadership skills by mentoring others and managing projects.

Yet, the answers to these questions do not have to be either/or. Both/and is also an option. In my enterprise solutions role I was both a manager and an individual contributor within strategic business analysis. You can choose to work with both internal business applications and external products, or to leverage an area of expertise across a wide range of industries.

The point of these questions is to help you clarify what kinds of opportunities light you up, not to limit your options. As always, you are in charge.

Expand Beyond Business Analysis

Your business analysis skill set is highly transferable and can open up opportunities in many different roles. Once you learn the business analysis mindset, you'll never look at a process or a software solution the same way again. This mindset brings immense value to many other professions:

- **Product owner.** This role on an agile software development team is a logical progression for a business analyst. Product owners are the main point of contact with the team regarding priorities. They often build and prioritize the product backlog, and may define the details of user stories in collaboration with stakeholders across the business. The primary difference between the product owner and business analyst is that the product owner has more decision-making authority. Business analysts who make this jump should be ready to take ownership of more decisions rather than facilitating decision-making.

- **Product manager.** The product manager is often responsible for one or more products or business lines and oversees the related product development, marketing, sales, and operations work. They conduct business analysis-adjacent work like building business cases and product vision statements and, like a product owner, have more ownership over the product.
- **Business architect.** Bridging the gap between an organization's strategy and execution, this role develops deliverables such as business capability models and value streams to represent a holistic and multidimensional view of the business.[11]
- **Information architect or content strategist.** These roles focus on the structural design and content organization in shared information environments, whether those are customer-facing systems like websites or internal systems like intranets.
- **User experience design.** Hoping to building more user-friendly software, UX roles often involve creating or managing wireframes, graphic design, usability studies, and deep process analysis or customer journey mapping.
- **Project management.** This role focuses on orchestrating the successful completion of projects through planning, team coordination, risk management, budget oversight, monitoring, and deployment.
- **Enterprise architect.** This role is responsible for establishing and overseeing the strategic information technology direction for an organization. It calls for a blend of deep understanding of the business and technical capabilities.

---

[11] For more detail, see Whynde Kuehn, *Strategy to Reality: Making the Impossible Possible for Business Architects, Change Makers and Strategy Execution Leaders* (Morgan James Publishing, 2023).

- **Data analyst or business intelligence analyst.** This role specializes in transforming raw data into actionable insights that inform business decisions, often using data visualization tools like Tableau or Power BI.
- **Business consultant.** Whether working independently or for a consulting company, consultants can provide a wide range of services, from practice development and training to hands-on business analysis work.[12]

This list merely scratches the surface of available opportunities. Don't be afraid to be creative and choose unusual paths. We've had course participants who went on to tackle roles as diverse as a sustainability consultant for a major energy company, a creative director at a major media company, and an independent technology consultant building custom solutions for small business clients.

The possibilities are endless, limited only by your enthusiasm and imagination. Your foundations in business analysis will always support you.

Define Your Career Path and Move Forward

This chapter has covered a lot: a typical success path, ways to leverage related roles, focus areas, and alternative career paths. It's a great deal to consider, and you don't have to figure this all out at once. But it's important that you decide on one to three steps you can take to advance your career.

The simple exercise that follows will help you reflect on everything you've learned in this book, create a plan of action, and establish a short-term plan that builds momentum toward your long-term goals.

Start by answering these four questions:

---

[12] For more detail, see Karl Wiegers, *Successful Business Analysis Consulting: Strategies and Tips for Going It Alone* (J. Ross Publishing, 2019).

- What work do you enjoy the most right now?
- What work do you enjoy the least right now?
- What's one new activity you are excited about or one skill you are looking to build?
- What resources do you have or need to do that?

Your most obvious next career steps are to eliminate and minimize what you enjoy the least, make room for the activities you enjoy the most, take on one new area of responsibility that excites you, and invest in the support you need (or accept the support that's already available to you).

It really can be that simple. You don't have to overthink this, although I know you want to!

It's a good idea to regularly reevaluate your responsibilities. Look at which ones are drawing you forward and which are pulling you back. Then eliminate, delegate, automate, or minimize the activities that have become stale or do not align with your goals and create room for the activities that will advance your career.

Let's make this real with an example. Beverly was a proven business analyst when she joined our program. Her challenge was that her manager saw her as a junior business analyst and nothing she did could shift that perception. She was stuck and frustrated. As she worked through her career development goals, she continued to develop her skills and do what she could to take on more meaningful contributions and challenging projects. She was inching forward and building new relationships outside her department.

Then, an instructor opportunity opened up at Bridging the Gap. I saw Beverly's potential, so I encouraged her to apply. Beverly earned the position, and started to contribute at a champion level while continuing in her full-time junior business analyst role. Her self-confidence soared, and she continued building relationships in her organization. About a year later, a new opportunity opened up in a different department. Beverly was hired into the role, with the title of Senior Business Analyst.

Let's look at another example. Manuel was a quality assurance engineer when he joined The Business Analyst Blueprint® training program. He wanted to shift his career toward solving problems. As soon as he joined, he updated his email signature to include "Business Analyst" as part of his job title, making it part of his identity and how he presented himself to colleagues. He volunteered to do requirements-related work on new projects so he could apply the new skills he was learning. Within months he was officially an enterprise platform business analyst. Manuel's career has taken many twists and turns. Today he is focused on building his technical skills and platform expertise, and his business analyst skills are still foundational to his success.

I could go on and on with these stories, and a common theme is that those who created momentum took action toward their career goals, starting exactly where they were at. That's what I want you to do with everything you've learned in this book—take action, apply what you've learned, and experience more career success as a result. You don't have to have it all figured out. Take one tip, one technique, one question, one practice, and experiment with it, either in your work or through a side project. Evaluate the results, learn from your experience, and then take the next step.

And as you take action, please be sure to let me know! Tag me or message me on LinkedIn—I absolutely love helping you celebrate your successes!

We sometimes think our careers are these big ideas that we've got to get perfect. We think we need a five-year strategic plan and crystal-clear career goals. If that works for you, then by all means get clear on where you are headed and make your goals specific, measurable, achievable, realistic, and timebound. It certainly won't hurt. But don't allow a fuzzy vision to keep you from acting on the opportunities in front of you right now. And don't substitute a clear vision for the practical action you need to move yourself forward, ignoring opportunities that may jump you ahead more quickly than your intended timeline.

Why am I so passionate about this? Because I believe with all my heart that business analysts make the world a better place. When you rise, we all win. The work you do matters and has an impact beyond the visible results you might see.

When you facilitate productive working meetings and everyone gets a voice, people find new meaning in their work and feel more engaged, which empowers everyone.

When you help the business automate repetitive, menial tasks, you free up your colleagues' time for more creative and meaningful work.

When you solve problems for your clients and customers, you enable them to create more value in new and exciting ways.

When you help your company implement a more sustainable and efficient process, you free up resources that would otherwise be wasted.

And perhaps most importantly, when you do work that matters to you in a way that energizes instead of depletes you, your entire life improves.

Business analysts make the world a better place, one project, one requirement, one change at a time. I want to live in a world that values business analysis, and where business analysis practices are at the core of every organizational change, because it will be a better world to live in, for all of us.

You may not see your impact, but I know it's real. This entire book has been about leading you on the path to creating more value in more efficient and productive ways. What will you do to act on what you've discovered?

✔ Success Strategy: Invest in Your Professional Development

Every successful business analyst I know is still learning and growing and plans to keep doing that. Career development is a journey, not a destination, and there are many, many resources available to support you along the way.

As you continue to explore and hone your business analysis skill set, consider the following ways of investing in your professional development:

- **Books.** Books are available on just about any topic and tend to be an affordable way to build new skills independently. Joining or starting a book club can be a great way to make new connections and deepen your perspective on the material.

- **Online resources.** There are a wide range of blogs, articles, podcasts, videos, live virtual events, webinars, and even LinkedIn thought leadership in the business analysis space, and new thought leaders are stepping in every day to share their knowledge and expertise. While it can be difficult to find exactly what you are looking for, and free resources may not be as deep as you'd like, online research is a great way to learn key concepts and get a feel for who you may want to work with more deeply as a trainer, mentor, or coach.

- **Courses and training programs.** Formal training supports a deeper exploration of a topic or skill set, often designed to support multiple learning styles. Consider programs that will support you with real-world experience, instructor feedback and answers to questions, and an ongoing community of professionals.

- **Professional associations.** IIBA is the community to join for webinars, articles, and comprehensive resources related to business analysis. Global membership has many benefits, and many major metropolitan areas have local chapters that host in-person and virtual events. This is a great way to connect with professionals in your local area. Also consider professional associations in any related roles, industries, or business applications you are excited about.
- **Study groups.** These tend to focus on preparing for a specific certification, and are often peer-facilitated. They can be a great way to meet like-minded professionals, learn from each others' experiences, and assimilate a large body of material.
- **Formal education.** A variety of undergraduate degrees, master's degrees, and certificate programs focus on business analysis and related disciplines. This tends to be the most costly way to build your skill set, both in terms of finances and time commitment, but may open up access to new connections and supply extra credibility.

As you can see, there are many ways to expose yourself to new knowledge and perspectives. Most professionals mix and match different learning opportunities to suit their goals, budget, and time.

As you consider different opportunities, consider the investment you are making in yourself and your career. Your business analysis skills have a long shelf-life, and will support you as you grow and expand into different roles. What feels like a big investment today could result in many new opportunities, more exciting work, and long-term career stability. One of our participants was starting a new position and felt a bit nervous about her formal business analyst skill set, even though she had a few years of experience in a business analyst role. She said that without investing in training she would be a stressed and frazzled business analyst. Instead, a year later she has delivered a few projects, built an expertise in cybersecurity, and feels confident talking to other business analysts about her work.

While personal investments are common, be sure not to overlook any resources you have available at your company, whether that's access to specific online learning tools, training budgets, or internal mentors for coaching and support. If you don't know, ask! Sometimes budgets are available under other categories, like consulting, that can be redirected into training, particularly if you can build a skill set that enables you to do work your company was expecting to outsource.

If your employer does provide funding, be sure to quantify the potential ROI not just for you and your career, but also for the organization. The company will benefit when you can make better contributions on your projects by saving stakeholder time, exploring new possibilities, finding more cost-effective solutions, and perhaps even saving outside consulting costs. Choose training in skill sets you can apply right away on the job will deliver an immediate impact.

❯❯ Next Steps

My goal with this book was to give you the exact insights you needed to make a positive impact on your projects and focus on value-creating work. If you have any questions, please reach out through our website or LinkedIn.

Here are some next steps to apply what you've learned:

- Identify your current career stage and use the next steps in that stage to identify the opportunities to move your career forward.

- Consider which related roles and responsibilities can broaden your skill set and unlock new opportunities for you in your career.
- Identify responsibilities that have become stale and look for ways to eliminate, delegate, automate, or minimize them.
- Explore different areas of focus, and use these insights to seek out opportunities that will take you in the direction you want to go, even if your vision isn't fully clear.
- Make an intentional investment in your professional development. Learn a new skill (or a collection of skills) and apply what you learn to expand your impact.

And always remember—you are in charge of your career. No one cares about your career as much as you do. Any ounce of energy you put into defining your goals and moving toward them will pay increasing dividends.

While this is the end of our journey together, in many ways you are just getting started. The doors are wide open for you, your business analysis skills, and your ability to leverage a structured process to increase your credibility and showcase your value.

Thank you for doing what you do. You are making the world a better place one project, one career move at a time.

Acknowldgments

A book like *The Value-Driven Business Analyst* is never the product of one individual. It takes a community of support, inspiration, and expertise to bring such a work to life. I am profoundly grateful to everyone who contributed to this journey.

First and foremost, to my family—David and our daughters—your unwavering love and encouragement have been my foundation. Thank you for believing in me and supporting me every step of the way. To Kurt and Emily, who, with David, witnessed the moment I decided to bring this book to life, and to both Emily and Monique for always asking about the book and continuing to be excited about the progress long after the project should have been interesting.

To the reviewers of this book, your insights and feedback were invaluable. You helped me refine and enhance the ideas shared here, ensuring they are practical and impactful for every reader. Thank you to Barbara Carkenord, Christina Lovelock, Elizabeth Harrin, Fabricio Laguna, Hannah Pearson-Coats, James Dean, Karl Wiegers, Meilir Page-Jones, Scott Ambler, Sophie Chen, Thea Soehren, Tracie Edwards, and Yonelly Guiterrez.

To every participant in our programs, thank you for your trust in the process and for striving to do your best in business analysis. A special thanks to those who allowed me to share your stories and examples in this book—your contributions bring these concepts to life.

To my incredible team of instructors over the years: Andrea Jones, Beverly Sudbury, Disha Trivedi, Doug Goldberg, Dr. Michael White, Nadine Millner, Paula Bell, and Toni V. Martin. Your challenges and insights have sharpened my thinking and brought out the careful nuances that enrich this work.

To my Durango 6 Mastermind—Callie King, Crystal Vilkaitis, Dr. Mary Barbera, Oonagh Duncan, and Stacey Murphy—your encouragement and insights over the last six years have been a source of inspiration and strength. This radiant group of women, each excelling in different business arenas, has always brought me back to a sense of true abundance.

To my B2B Mastermind—Ada Deferrari, Craig Peterson, Erik Solbakken, May Busch, and Walt Hampton—thank you for being my trusted confidants. For over five years, we've shared our deepest hardships and celebrated our biggest victories. Your profound understanding of my work and life has been a gift of the highest order.

To Richelle Fredson, who coached me through crafting a compelling book proposal—your guidance enabled me to clarify my vision and secure invaluable industry feedback before writing a single word.

To every potential agent and publisher representative I spoke with, thank you for your candid feedback and suggestions, which informed my creative process and ultimately helped me shape and organize the work.

To the International Institute of Business Analysis (IIBA), its founders, volunteers, members, employees, and contributors—your dedication has cultivated business analysis as a respected, credible profession. I am honored to be part of this thriving community.

To DeAnna Burghart, my editor, for your meticulous attention to detail and ability to bring clarity to the content—your expertise is woven into every page—and to Nick Zelinger for bringing visual appeal to this book through your thoughtful design and cover work—thank you for making it inviting and accessible.

And finally, to you, the reader. This book is for you and because of you. Your commitment to doing YOUR best in business analysis will continue to create value in ways that inspire me every day. Thank you for doing your best in business analysis.

www.ingramcontent.com/pod-product-compliance
Lightning Source LLC
Chambersburg PA
CBHW061137220326
41599CB00025B/4270